Back to Basics™

YEARS 2 & 3

ADDITION AND SUBTRACTION

Do you need to know the basics of addition and subtraction? Let's learn about them together.

Parents and carers are encouraged to read the explanation and practice sections with their child.

Ann Baker

Illustrated by
Janice Bowles

About this book

Each unit in this book begins with a brief **explanation** of a concept or a strategy. You are encouraged to read this explanation with your child and, where appropriate, to use everyday materials and examples to give meaning to the concepts.

We practise is a worked example for you and your child to discuss together, paying particular attention to the thinking processes required to understand the concept or apply the strategy.

You practise gives your child the opportunity to practise the concept or strategy. It also indicates how well your child understands the new material and often includes problem-solving questions to ensure that your child has mastered the concept or strategy.

If further support is required, you and your child's teacher can devise a plan to ensure that all the basic concepts are fully understood and consolidated.

The **Tests** at the end of the book are provided to check that the concepts are fully understood. Test 1 can be done after units 1–10 are completed and Test 2 when the book is finished.

Meet 'BOB' – Back Of the Book

At the end of each unit, BOB reminds your child to go to the Answers section at the back of the book.

Mathematical Content

This book has been designed to cover the concepts of addition and subtraction that your child will encounter in **Year 2** and **Year 3**. The units provide a comprehensive coverage of the following Key Topics from the **Australian Curriculum: Mathematics**.

Australian Curriculum : Mathematics

YEAR 2

Explore the connection between addition and subtraction (ACMNA029)
Solve simple addition and subtraction problems using a range of efficient mental and written strategies (ACMNA030)
Solve problems by using number sentences for addition or subtraction (ACMNA036)

YEAR 3

Recognise and explain the connection between addition and subtraction (ACMNA054)
Recall addition facts for single-digit numbers and related subtraction facts to develop increasingly efficient mental strategies for computation (ACMNA055)
Describe, continue, and create number patterns resulting from performing addition or subtraction (ACMNA060)

Contents & Checklist

WRITING and TALKING ABOUT ADDITION & SUBTRACTION

Addition

3 + 4 = 7 is a number sentence.

The **plus** sign, **+**, means **add** the numbers in an equation.

There are other words that have the same meaning as add.

3 **and** 4 **more**

3 **plus** 4

So you need to watch out for words that tell you that addition is required.

The word **makes** is also a word that is used in addition.

2 plus 2 **makes** 4

When a question asks you to **Find the total ...**, this also means that you need to **add** to find the answer.

Subtraction

6 – 3 = 3 is also a number sentence.

The minus sign, **–**, means **subtract** the second number from the first in an equation.

There are other words that have the same meaning as subtract.

6 **minus** 3

6 **take away** 3

Other words that tell you a question is a subtraction are **leaves** and **left**.

7 take away 2 **leaves** 5

If you take away 2 from 7, how many are **left**?

Equals

In an equation, the numbers on one side of an equals sign, **=**, must have the same value as, or **balance**, the numbers on the other side.

8 **balances** 3 + 5, so you can write this fact as an equation 8 = 3 + 5

3 + 5 **balances** 2 + 6, so you can write this fact as an equation 3 + 5 = 6 + 2

Watch out! The equals sign is usually followed by an answer, but not always. So think carefully about what the equals sign means and remember that it does not mean add or subtract.

GAME CARD IDEAS

Cut out the game cards – they will last longer if they are laminated. Here are some games for you to try.

Highest/Lowest Total

To introduce this game use only single-digit cards. Before each round decide whether to go for highest or lowest total.

On their turn, players take two cards and add them together. The player with the highest/lowest total wins a point. When the cards run out, the player with the highest score wins the game.

As players become more skilled, three or even four cards can be taken at a time and then returned to the bottom of the pile to keep the game going.

The game can also be played as a subtraction game with just the single-digit cards. Players take two cards and subtract the lower number from the higher number. In this case playing for lowest answer is the most fun.

As progress is made, both games can be played with just the 10s cards. Gradually change from taking one card from the single-digit pile and one from the 10s pile and carrying out an addition or subtraction, to players randomly selecting from a mix of all cards.

BEAT THE CALCULATOR

A game for 3 or more players.

One player calls out an addition or subtraction using the numbers on the cards. One player enters the sum on the calculator and the other player tries to answer before the calculator has the answer.

As you play, encourage your child to mentally compute using the strategies presented in this book.

Provide paper for your child to write any calculations that cannot be carried out mentally (yet).

Race to 50 or Race to 0

Race to 50 or Race to 0 can be played with just the single-digit cards.

As the name suggests, players take a card on their turn and keep a running total. First player to reach 50 or 0 or bust wins the game.

NOTE: Games are meant to be fun and provide practice without stress. It is recommended that you stop playing while you are still having fun and then your child will want to play again another time.

UNIT 1 COUNT ON and COUNT BACK

There are 3 apples in one bowl and 2 apples in another bowl. How many apples altogether?

To solve this addition you do not need to count all the apples, you can just **count on** from the larger number. Start with the 3 and **count on** 2 more, like this:

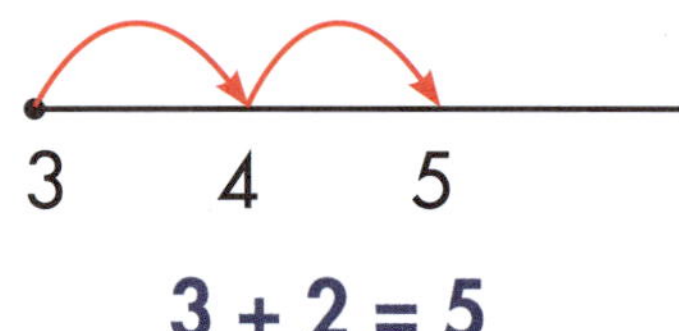

3 4 5

3 + 2 = 5

The numbers 2, 3 and 5 make a **fact family**.

2 + 3 = 5 5 − 2 = 3
3 + 2 = 5 5 − 3 = 2

Did you notice that both problems use the same numbers but in a different order?

There are 5 apples in a bowl and then 2 are eaten. How many apples are left in the bowl?

You can **count back** to solve this problem. Start at 5 and **count back** 2, like this:

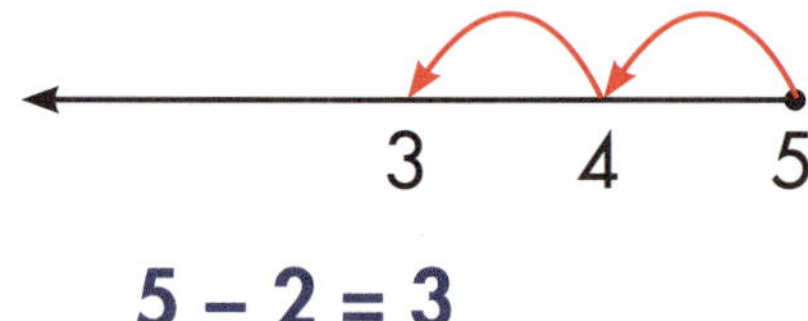

3 4 5

5 − 2 = 3

We practise

4 oranges in a bowl and 3 more are added. How many oranges altogether?
Solve this addition by counting on using a number line.

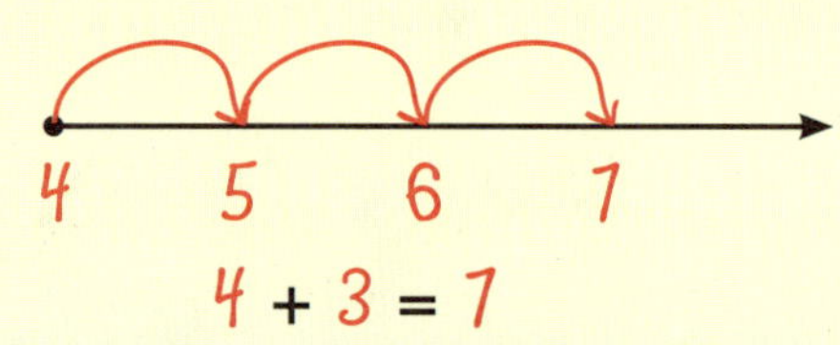

7 oranges in a bag, but 3 fell out. How many oranges left in the bag?
Solve this addition by counting back using a number line.

You practise

Solve each addition problem by counting on using an empty number line.

1 5 birds and 1 more came along. How many birds altogether?

5 + 1 = ______

Remember to **count on** from the larger number every time.

2 4 apples in a bowl and 3 more are added.
How many apples altogether?

4 + 3 = ______

3 2 fish and 5 more swim by. How many fish altogether?

2 + 5 = ______

Solve each subtraction problem by counting back using an empty number line.

4 6 apples in a bowl and 3 are eaten. How many apples left?

6 − 3 = ______

Remember to **count back** from the larger number, but don't include it in the count.

5 7 birds in the nest and 2 fly away. How many birds left?

7 − 2 = ______

6 8 fish in a school and 3 swim away. How many fish left?

8 − 3 = ______

BOB time!

DOUBLES and NEAR DOUBLES FOR ADDITION

When you throw two dice for a game it is possible to throw the same number on both dice. Two dice showing the same number is called a **double**.

4 + 4 = 8

4 + 4 is a double.

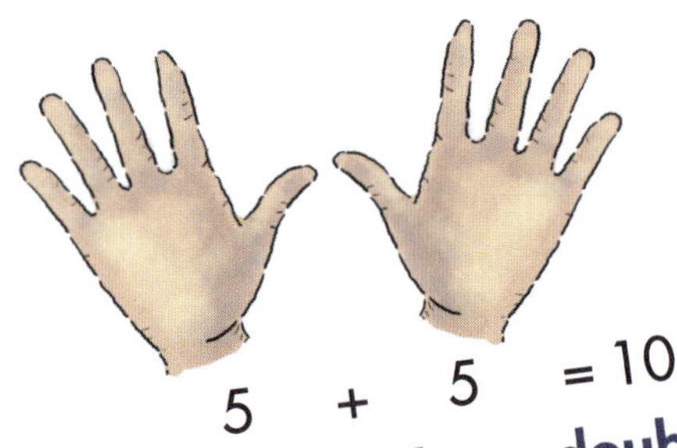

5 + 5 = 10

5 + 5 is also a double.

When you know doubles, working out **near doubles** is easy.

4 and 5 are close to

or to

So for 4 + 5 you can think **double.**

4 + 4 + 1 = 9 or 5 + 5 − 1 = 9

We practise

Complete these doubles facts.

1 + 1 = 2	4 + 4 = 8
2 + 2 = 4	5 + 5 = 10
3 + 3 = 6	6 + 6 = 12

Which doubles could you use to find the answer to 3 + 4?

3 + 3 + 1 = 7

4 + 4 − 1 = 7

You practise Complete these doubles facts as fast as you can.

1 5 + 5 = ____

4 ____ + ____ = 4

2 4 + ____ = 8

5 ____ + ____ = 6

3 ____ + 6 = 12

6 7 + ____ = 14

You practise Which doubles could you use to find the answer to these near doubles?

7 4 + 5

____ + ____ + 1 = ____

____ + ____ − 1 = ____

8 3 + 4

____ + ____ + 1 = ____

____ + ____ − 1 = ____

9 5 + 6

____ + ____ + 1 = ____

____ + ____ − 1 = ____

10 6 + 7

____ + ____ + 1 = ____

____ + ____ − 1 = ____

UNIT 3 RAINBOW FACTS for ADDITION

The pairs of numbers that add up to 10 can be joined to make a rainbow like this.

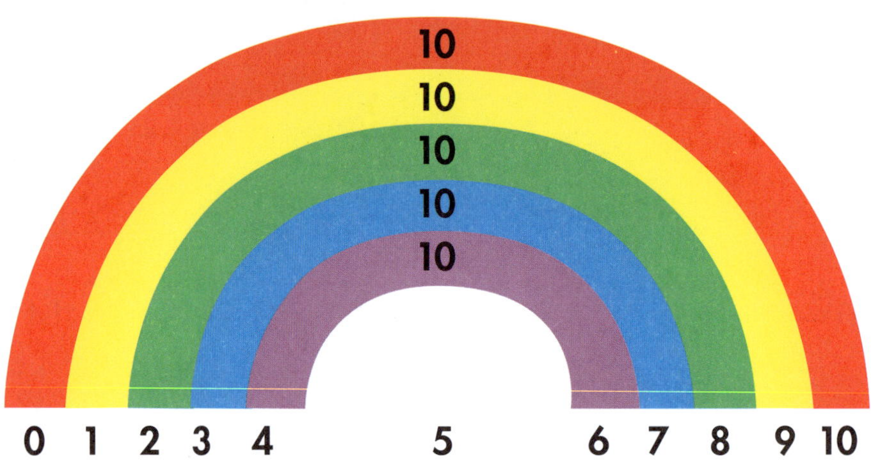

Start on **0** and move your finger along the rainbow until you reach the other end.

This tells you that 0 + 10 = 10.

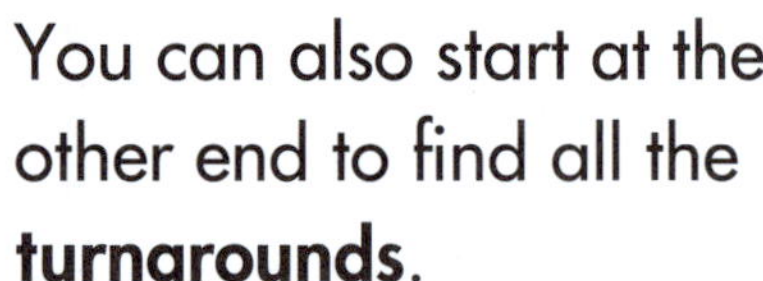

This time start at **3** and follow the rainbow until you come to **7**.

This tells you that 3 + 7 = 10.

Now try starting with the other numbers. You will find all the **pairs** of numbers that **add** up to **10**.

You can also start at the other end to find all the **turnarounds**.

For example, put your finger on **7** and then follow the rainbow back to **3**.

This tells you that 7 + 3 = 10.

We practise

Use the rainbow to complete these rainbow facts.

3 + 7 = 10

4 + 6 = 10

1 + 9 = 10

Use the rainbow to complete these rainbow facts and their turnarounds.

2 + 8 = 10   4 + 6 = 10

8 + 2 = 10   6 + 4 = 10

You practise Use the rainbow to complete these rainbow facts.

 3 + ______ = 10

 1 + ______ = 10

 4 + ______ = 10

 2 + ______ = 10

 ______ + 7 = 10

10
10
10
10
10

0 1 2 3 4 5 6 7 8 9 10

You practise Use the rainbow to complete these rainbow facts and their turnarounds.

 0 + ______ = 10 ______ + 0 = 10

 3 + ______ = 10 ______ + 3 = 10

 2 + ______ = 10 ______ + 2 = 10

 4 + ______ = 10 ______ + 4 = 10

 1 + ______ = 10 ______ + 1 = 10

If you use the turnarounds, there is no need to work the answer out again.

UNIT 4

ZERO is a FRIENDLY NUMBER

Any number that ends in a 0 is called a **friendly number** because it is easy to add to.

Adding zero to a number is easy.

2 + 0 = 2 is the same as saying:

I have 2 marbles in one hand and none in the other hand, so I only have 2 marbles altogether.

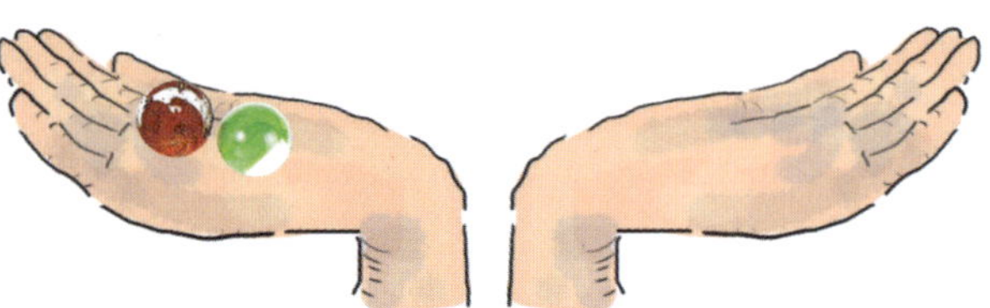

2 marbles 0 marbles

Watch what happens when you add zero to a number:

3 + 0 = 3

0 + 4 = 4

The number does not change because you are adding 0, which is **nothing**.

Now watch what happens when you add a friendly number, such as 10, to a number:

10 + 3 = 13

10 + 4 = 14

Look out for other friendly numbers, such as 20 and 50:

20 + 3 = 23

50 + 4 = 54

We practise

Complete these zero addition facts.

0 + 6 = 6

7 + 0 = 7

Complete these friendly number addition facts.

10 + 3 = 13

4 + 20 = 24

You practise Complete these zero addition facts.

 5 + 0 = ______

 8 + 0 = ______

 3 + 0 = ______

 0 + 4 = ______

 0 + 6 = ______

Zeros are so friendly!

You practise Complete these friendly number addition facts.

 10 + 6 = ______

 10 + 9 = ______

 8 + 20 = ______

 4 + 30 = ______

 50 + 3 = ______

You may need to do a turnaround before you add to the friendly number.

BOB time!

UNIT 5

RAINBOW FACTS for SUBTRACTION

You can use **rainbow facts** for **subtraction** as well as for **addition**.

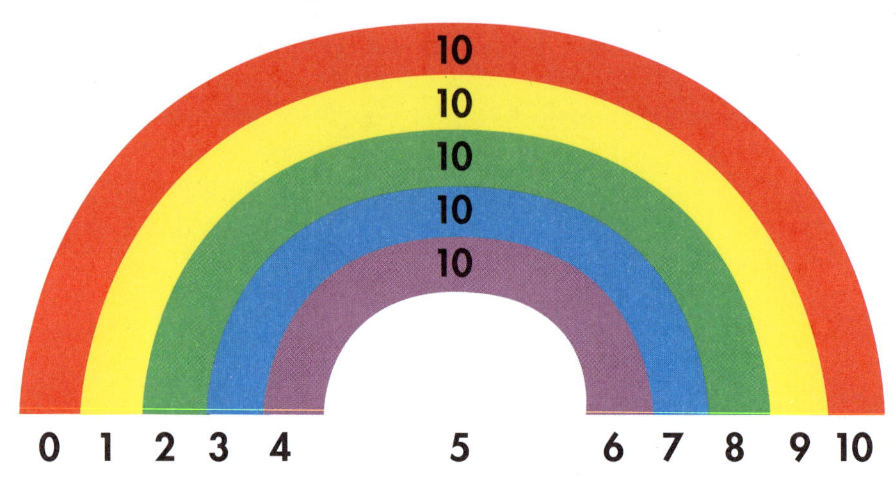

If you know your addition rainbow facts, subtracting from 10 is easy.

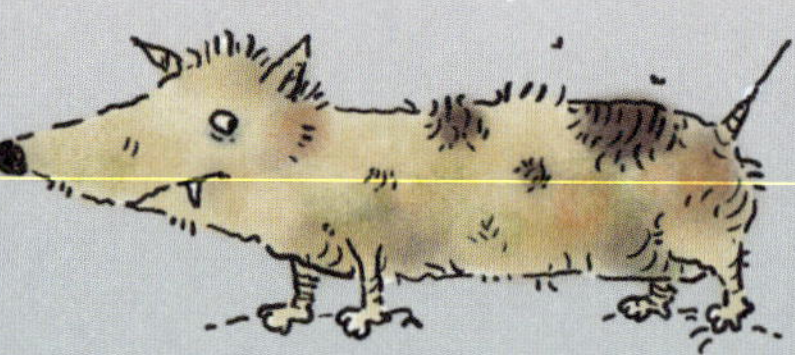

To work out 10 – 7, think:

What is the other number in the rainbow pair that goes with 7 to make 10?

Put your finger on 7 and follow it along the rainbow to 3.

10 – 7 = 3

3 7

For 10 – 2, think:

What is the other number that goes with 2 to make 10?

Put your finger on the 2 and follow it along the rainbow to 8.

10 – 2 = 8

2 8

Every addition fact in the rainbow can help you with two subtraction facts. For example:

7 + 3 = 10 helps with

10 – 7 = 3 and **10 – 3 = 7**

We practise

Use the rainbow to work out 10 – 6.

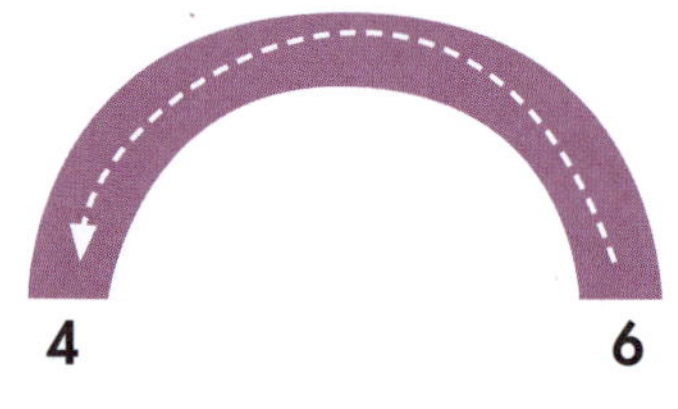

10 – 6 = 4

Which addition rainbow fact helps with 10 – 4?

4 + 6 = 10

10 – 4 = 6

You practise Use the rainbow to work out these subtraction facts.

1. 10 − 3 = ______

2. 10 − 4 = ______

3. 10 − 1 = ______

4. 10 − 2 = ______

5. 20 − 4 = ______

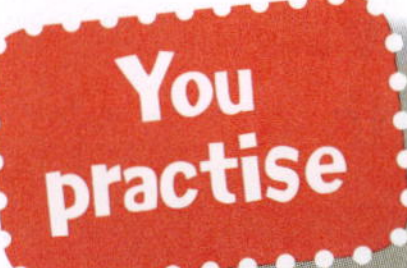

Which addition rainbow fact helps you work out each subtraction fact?

	Subtraction	Rainbow fact
 6	10 − 8 = ______	______ + ______ = 10
 7	20 − 3 = ______	______ + ______ = 10
 8	30 − 6 = ______	______ + ______ = 10
 9	40 − 9 = ______	______ + ______ = 10
 10	50 − 7 = ______	______ + ______ = 10

Remember to think of the other number in the rainbow pair.

DOUBLES and NEAR DOUBLES for SUBTRACTION

6 is half of 12 so 12 – 6 = 6.

If you know **double 6 is 12**, then you can easily find **12 – 6**.

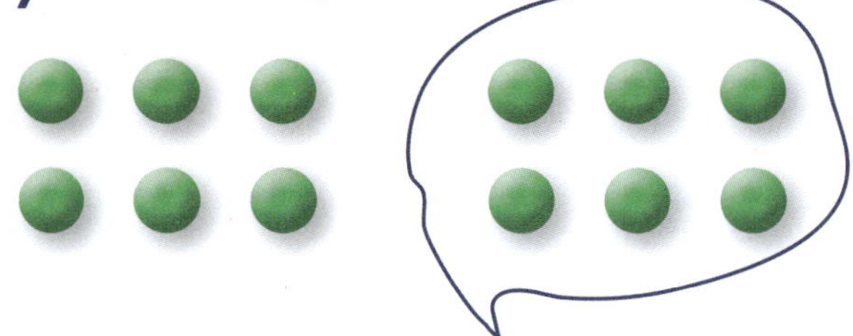

6 + 6 = 12 take away 6 → 12 – 6 = 6

You can easily find **9 – 4** if you know the near double **4 + 5 = 9** (think 4 + 4 + 1).

5 + 4 = 9 take away 4 → 9 – 4 = 5

Can you explain in your own words how near doubles work for subtraction? Draw pictures if you need to.

Fact families help with subtraction: **5 + 4 = 9**, so **9 – 4 = 5.**

We practise

Which double fact helps you work out 8 – 4? What is the answer?

4 + 4 = 8

8 – 4 = 4

Which near double helps you work out 7 – 3? What is the answer?

4 + 3 = 7

7 – 3 = 4

You practise

Which double fact helps you work out each subtraction fact?

 10 – 5 = ______ ______ + ______ = ______

 6 – 3 = ______ ______ + ______ = ______

 12 – 6 = ______ ______ + ______ = ______

 14 – 7 = ______ ______ + ______ = ______

 20 – 10 = ______ ______ + ______ = ______

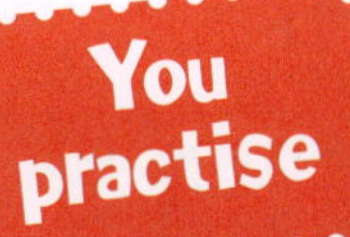

Which near double helps you work out each subtraction fact?

 5 – 2 = ______ ______ + ______ = ______

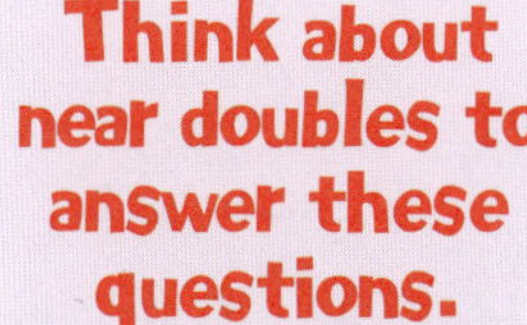

 9 – 4 = ______ ______ + ______ = ______

 11 – 6 = ______ ______ + ______ = ______

 19 – 9 = ______ ______ + ______ = ______

 21 – 10 = ______ ______ + ______ = ______

BRIDGE THROUGH 10

You know how easy it is to add to 10, which is a friendly number. You can also use 10 to help with other additions.

For example, to work out **9 + 4** follow these steps:

Step 1 Split 4 into 1 + 3

Step 2 9 + 1 = 10

Step 3 10 + 3 = 13

This is shown on the **bridge** diagram below.

Did you notice that **8 + 2 + 3 = 13** and **13 – 3 – 2 = 8** are related?

You can also use the bridge for subtraction, but going backwards. For example, **13 – 5** on the bridge looks like this:

Here the 5 is split into 3 and 2 because 13 – 3 is 10 and 2 less is 8.

We practise

Complete the bridge to show how to work out 9 + 6.

Complete the bridge to show how to work out 15 – 6.

You practise Complete the bridge to show how you would work out each addition.

1 7 + 9

2 7 + 5

3 8 + 6

You practise Complete the bridge to show how you would work out each subtraction.

4 13 – 9

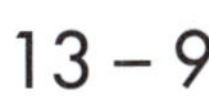

5 16 – 7

6 21 – 8

Remember to split the number you are subtracting so that the first step takes you back to a 10.

ADDING STRINGS of NUMBERS

It is easy to add strings of numbers if you think smart and use the strategies that you have already learnt.

Look at this string of numbers.

3 + 4 + 7 + 6

This string of numbers is not easy to add. But it will be easier if you rearrange them so that the **rainbow pairs** are together.

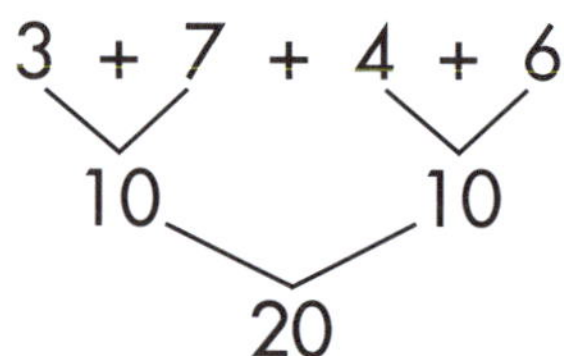

Chunking the rainbow pairs together makes 10 and then **doubling** 10 makes 20.

Finding numbers that add to 10 always makes adding easier.

Now try adding this string.

5 + 3 + 4 + 3

Can you spot a way of making 10? How about:

3 + 3 + 4 + 5

6

10

15

Double 3 is 6, adding 4 makes 10, and 5 is easy to add onto a friendly number.

We practise

Rearrange the numbers in 3 + 2 + 7 + 3 to find a 10 and show the chunking steps.

7 + 3 + 3 + 2

10 5

15

Rearrange the numbers in 9 + 2 + 3 + 6 for easy addition and use chunking to find the total.

9 + 6 + 3 + 2

15

18

20

You practise

Rearrange each number string to find a 10 and show the chunking steps.

1. 2 + 7 + 8 + 1

+ + +

2. 6 + 3 + 4 + 5

+ + +

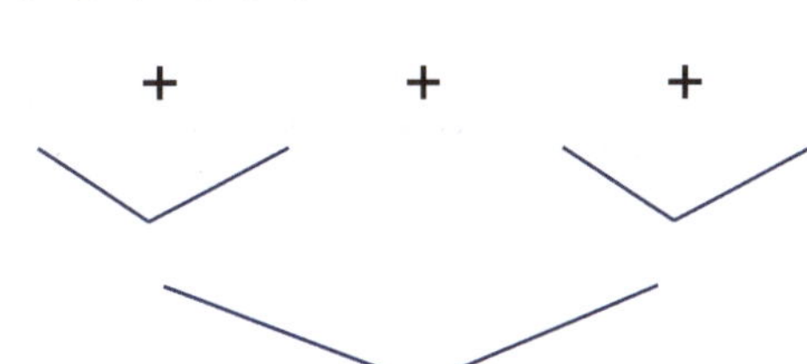

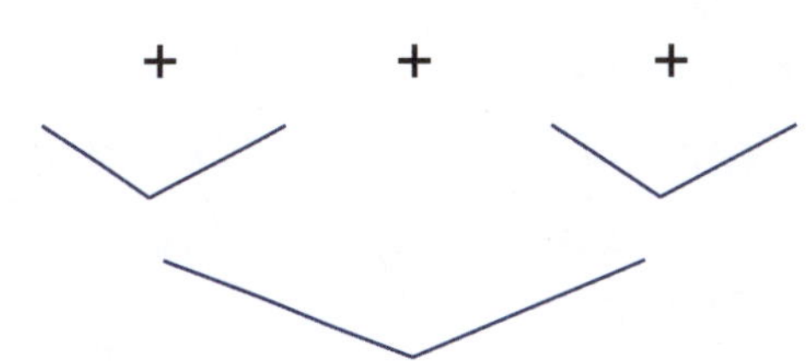

3. 1 + 7 + 2 + 9

+ + +

4. 6 + 3 + 1 + 7

+ + +

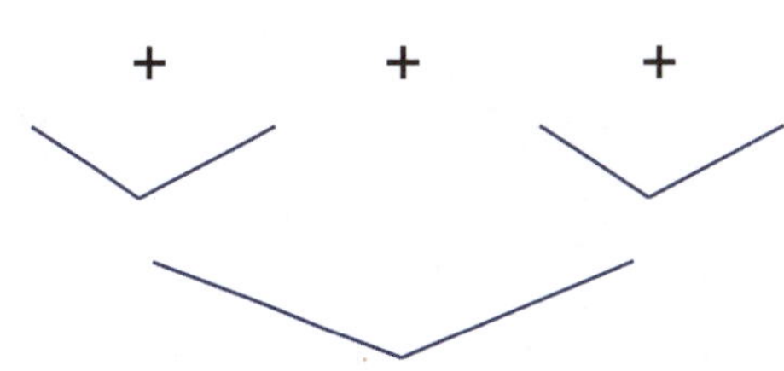

Rearrange each number string for easy addition and use chunking to find the total.

5. 5 + 8 + 3 + 4

+ + +

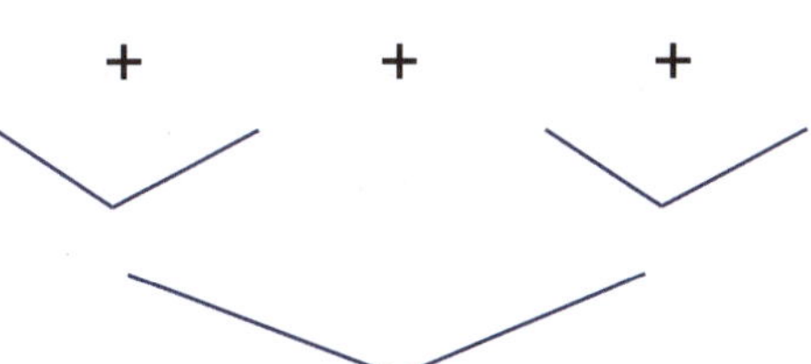

6. 3 + 5 + 4 + 2

+ + +

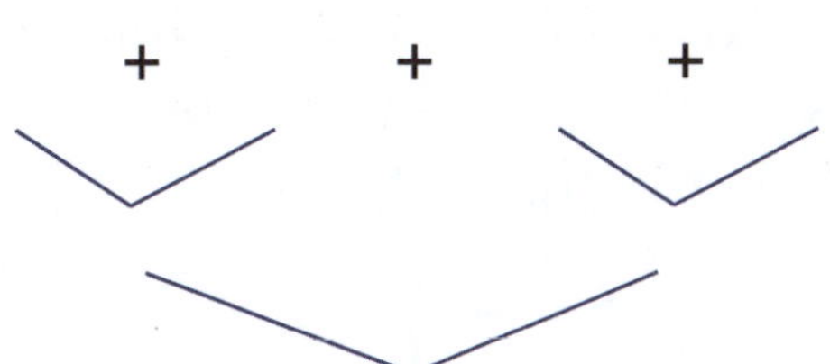

7. 2 + 7 + 4 + 5

+ + +

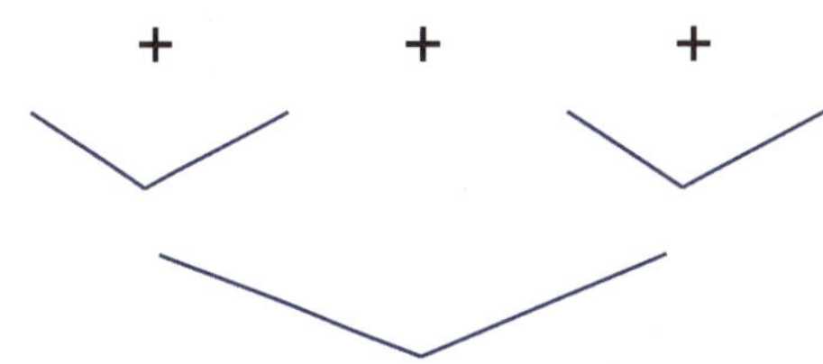

8. 9 + 5 + 3 + 6

+ + +

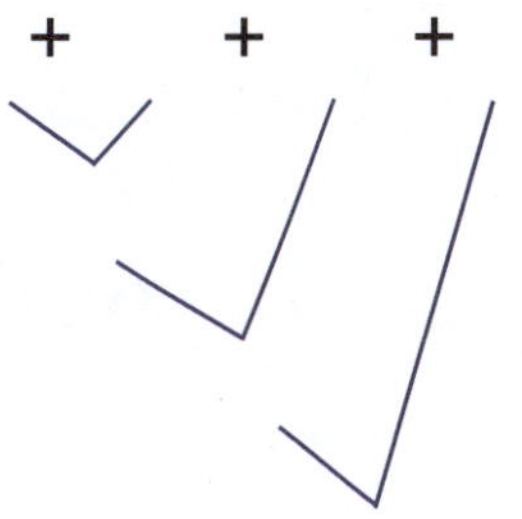

You might need to bridge the 10s first.

BOB time!

UNIT 9 ADDITION PROBLEMS

Remember to ask yourself: What is the unknown? Is it the **result**, the **start** or the **change** that I have to find?

Sometimes an addition problem simply needs an answer (or result).

For example:

If you have 3 marbles in one bag and 2 marbles in another bag, how many marbles altogether?

3 + 2

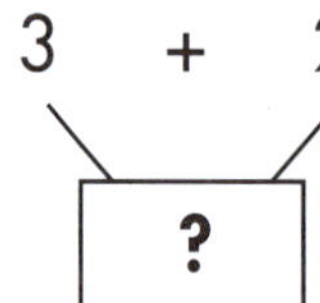

the **result** is unknown

But there are other types of addition problems that can catch you out.

Look at these two examples.

If you have 5 marbles altogether, with 3 in the first bag, how many are in the second bag?

3 + ?

5

the **change** is unknown

If you have 5 marbles altogether, with 2 marbles in the second bag, how many marbles are in the first bag?

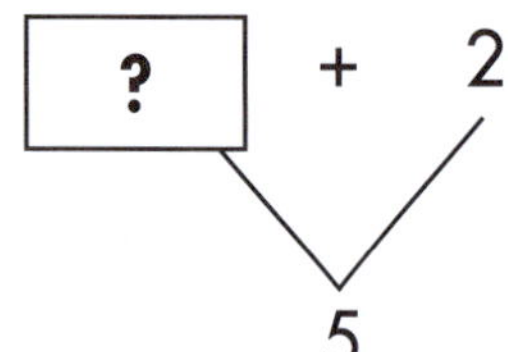

the **start** is unknown

We practise

If you have 9 marbles, with 6 in the first bag, how many are in the second bag?

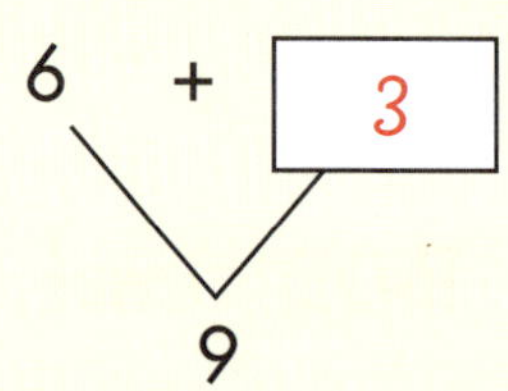

If you have 9 marbles altogether, with 3 in one bag, how many in the other? What is the unknown?

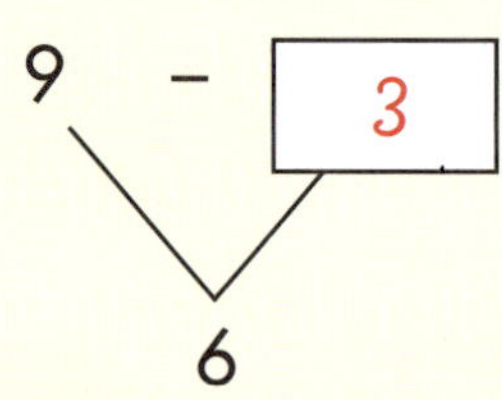

The change is unknown

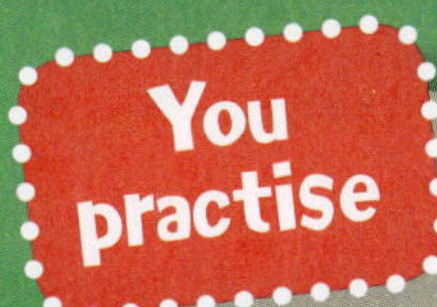

Solve each addition problem.

There are 5 apples in one bowl,
and 8 apples altogether.
How many apples in the other bowl?

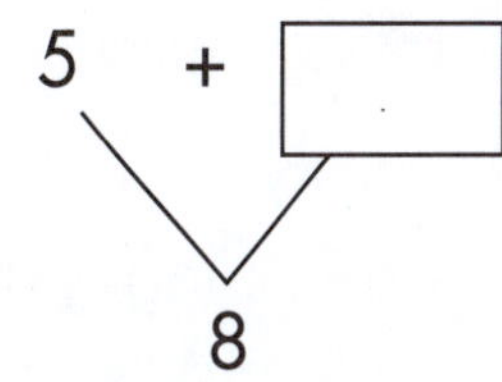

My friend gave me 8 marbles.
Now I have 11 marbles.
How many marbles did I have at the start?

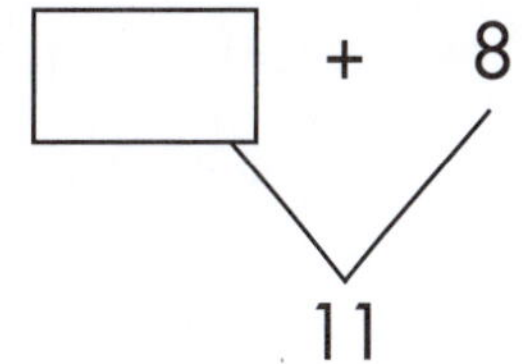

I started with 6 marbles and won 5 more.
How many marbles do I have now?

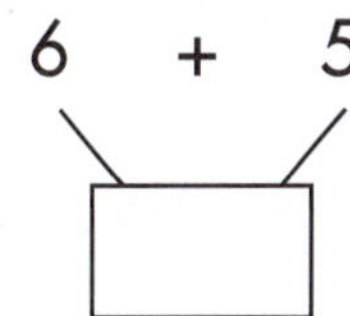

Solve each addition problem and write what is unknown.

5 + ☐
13

the ________________ is unknown

9 + 19
☐

the ________________ is unknown

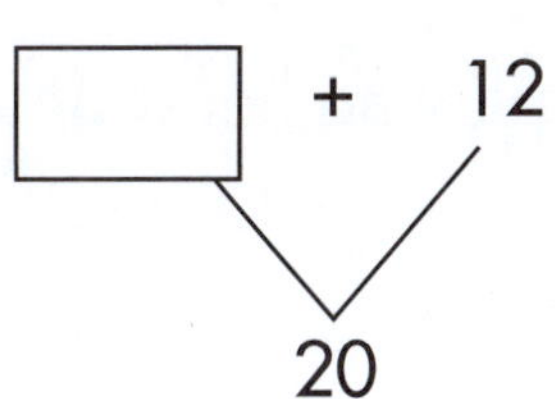

the ________________ is unknown

BOB time!

PROBLEM SOLVING

How many marbles?

Clare, Jake, Matty and Tsai brought their marbles ready for a game. Clare has 7 marbles, Jake has 5, Tsiai has 5 and poor Matty has only 3.
"That's not enough marbles," Matty says.
"We should get some more."
How many marbles do they have altogether?

Notice that the important information is highlighted in blue and what has to be found out is highlighted in pink.

Follow these steps to solve the problem.

Step 1 Write the numbers in sequence as an addition sentence.

7 + 5 + 5 + 3

Step 2 If necessary, rearrange the numbers to make them easy to add.

7 + 3 + 5 + 5

Step 3 Show the chunking steps.

7 + 3 + 5 + 5
10 10
20

Answer: They have 20 marbles altogether.

Remember that making 10s is always a smart way to add.

Remember to write the answer as a sentence.

Highlight the important information and what you have to find out in this problem and then work out the answer.

Clare started with 11 marbles and lost 5 while playing her round. How many marbles does Clare have left?

11 – 5 (think near double 5 + 5 + 1 = 11)

Answer: Clare has 6 marbles left.

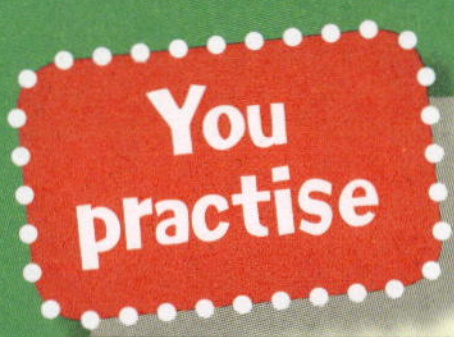

Highlight the important information and solve the problems.

1. There are four tubs of pencils, one with 6, one with 7, one with 4 and another with 5. "So how many pencils altogether?" the teacher asked.

____

Remember to use the smart strategies you have been learning and to look for 10s.

2. "I had 12 marbles, but lost 6. How many do I have now?" Matty asked. ______________________________

3. The chickens laid 8 eggs on Monday, 8 on Tuesday and 4 on Wednesday. "How many eggs altogether?" the children asked.

____

4. "I have 9 apples and need 5 to make a pie. How many will I have left?" Clare's mum asked. ______________________________

5. There are 13 apples in two bowls. If there are 6 in one bowl, then how many are in the other bowl? ______________________________

6. Clare started with 11 marbles and lost 3 in the first game and 2 in the next game. How many marbles does she have left?

____

7. "I need 12 eggs for the cakes I am baking. I have 4 eggs so how many more do I need?" the baker asked. ______________________________

8. "I won!" Matty said. "I threw 6, 6, 4 and 5 on the dice." "No, I won!" Clare said. "I threw 5, 5, 6 and 4." Who actually won the dice game?

____

9. Clare threw 3, 4, 5 and 6 and Matty threw 3, 5, 6 and 2 in the dice game. Who won and by how much? ______________________________

10. Clare spent $5 on a toy, $7 on a notebook, $2 on a pencil and $2 on an eraser. How much did she spend? ______________________________

BOB time!

UNIT 11

ADDING 10s

All numbers ending in zero are **friendly numbers** because they are easy to add.

Adding numbers that end in zero is easy.

For example, if you don't instantly know the answer to **30 + 20**, you can work it out by **counting on** in 10s.

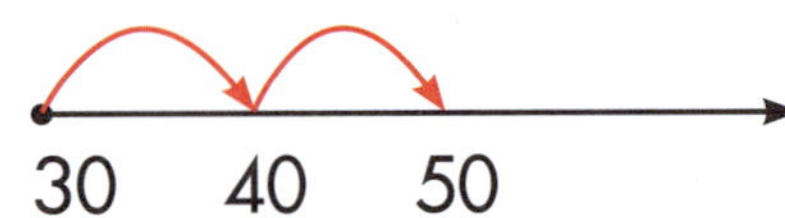

Doubles, **near doubles** and **rainbow facts** can also help you add 10s. Look at these examples.

For **40 + 40** think 4 + 4.

Double 4 is 8, so double 40 must be 80.

For **40 + 50** think 4 + 5. The **near double** is 4 + 4 + 1 = 9, so 40 + 50 must be 90.

For **70 + 30** the **rainbow fact** is 7 + 3 = 10, so 70 + 30 must be 100.

Adding 10s to a single digit number is easy too.

Look at these additions and you will see a pattern.

3 + 10 = 13

3 + 20 = 23

3 + 30 = 33

3 + 40 = 43

Did you notice that the single digit number has replaced the zero each time? How easy is that?

We practise

Complete each addition and name the related strategy.

50 + 20 = 70 count on

60 + 40 = 100 rainbow fact

30 + 30 = 60 double

40 + 30 = 70 near double

Complete each friendly number addition.

20 + 4 = 24

5 + 30 = 35

50 + 6 = 56

80 + 8 = 88

Back to Basics

ADDITION & SUBTRACTION

YEARS 2 and 3

Back to Basics

ADDITION & SUBTRACTION

YEARS 2 and 3

Back to Basics

ADDITION & SUBTRACTION

YEARS 2 and 3

Back to Basics

ADDITION & SUBTRACTION

YEARS 2 and 3

Back to Basics

ADDITION & SUBTRACTION

YEARS 2 and 3

Back to Basics

ADDITION & SUBTRACTION

YEARS 2 and 3

Back to Basics

ADDITION & SUBTRACTION

YEARS 2 and 3

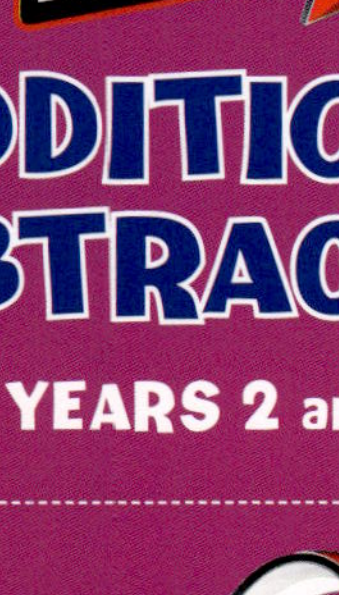

Back to Basics

ADDITION & SUBTRACTION

YEARS 2 and 3

Back to Basics

ADDITION & SUBTRACTION

YEARS 2 and 3

Back to Basics

ADDITION & SUBTRACTION

YEARS 2 and 3

Back to Basics

ADDITION & SUBTRACTION

YEARS 2 and 3

Back to Basics

ADDITION & SUBTRACTION

YEARS 2 and 3

Back to Basics

ADDITION & SUBTRACTION

YEARS 2 and 3

Back to Basics

ADDITION & SUBTRACTION

YEARS 2 and 3

Back to Basics

ADDITION & SUBTRACTION

YEARS 2 and 3

Back to Basics

ADDITION & SUBTRACTION

YEARS 2 and 3

1	2	3	4
5	6	7	8
9	10	20	30
40	50	60	70

80	90	100	40
1	2	3	4
5	6	7	8
9	10	20	30

ADDITION & SUBTRACTION

YEARS 2 and 3

ADDITION & SUBTRACTION
YEARS 2 and 3

ADDITION & SUBTRACTION
YEARS 2 and 3

ADDITION & SUBTRACTION
YEARS 2 and 3

ADDITION & SUBTRACTION
YEARS 2 and 3
ADDITION & SUBTRACTION
YEARS 2 and 3
ADDITION & SUBTRACTION
YEARS 2 and 3
ADDITION & SUBTRACTION
YEARS 2 and 3
ADDITION & SUBTRACTION
YEARS 2 and 3

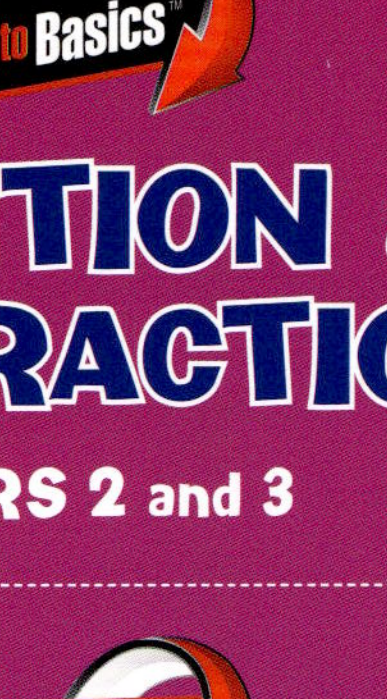

ADDITION & SUBTRACTION
YEARS 2 and 3
ADDITION & SUBTRACTION
YEARS 2 and 3
ADDITION & SUBTRACTION
YEARS 2 and 3
ADDITION & SUBTRACTION
YEARS 2 and 3

ADDITION & SUBTRACTION
YEARS 2 and 3
ADDITION & SUBTRACTION
YEARS 2 and 3
ADDITION & SUBTRACTION
YEARS 2 and 3

ADDITION & SUBTRACTION
YEARS 2 and 3

You practise

Complete each addition and name the related strategy.

 40 + 20 = _____ ____________________

 30 + 70 = _____ ____________________

 40 + 40 = _____ ____________________

 50 + 40 = _____ ____________________

5 30 + _____ = 70 ____________________

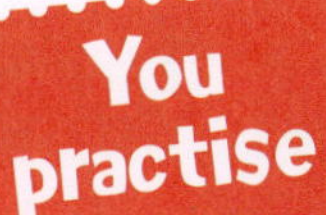

Complete each friendly number addition.

 30 + 6 = _____

 7 + 70 = _____

 5 + 10 = _____

 _____ + 30 = 36

 6 + _____ = 56

Remember, it's easy to add to a friendly number.

BOB time!

UNIT 12 ADDING 10s and 1s

Many of the different ways to add 10s and 1s are based on number splitting.

For example, **25 + 36** can be added in two different ways.

Think of splitting 25 into two chunks, 20 and 5, and 36 into 30 and 6. Then you can add the chunks.

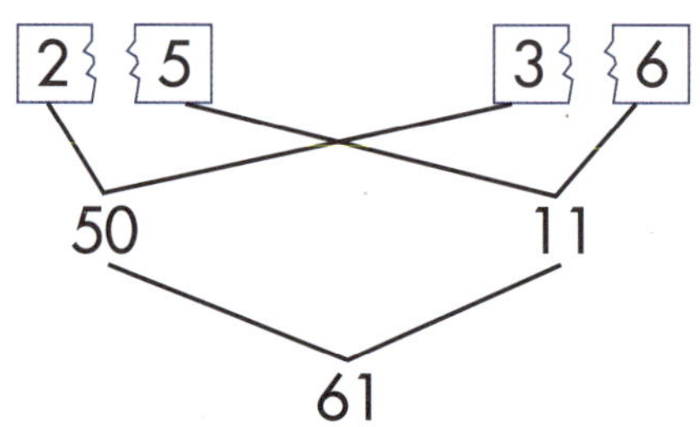

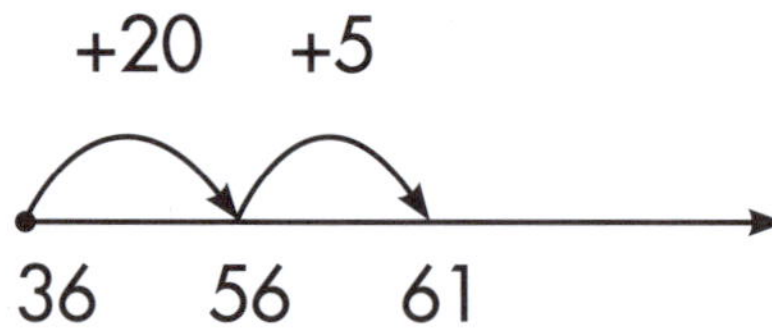

You can also add the numbers using an empty number line.

Sometimes it is best to start from the larger number, so start from 36 and then split 25 into 20 and 5, like this:

+20 +5

36 56 61

We practise

Show how to add 44 + 37 using chunking.

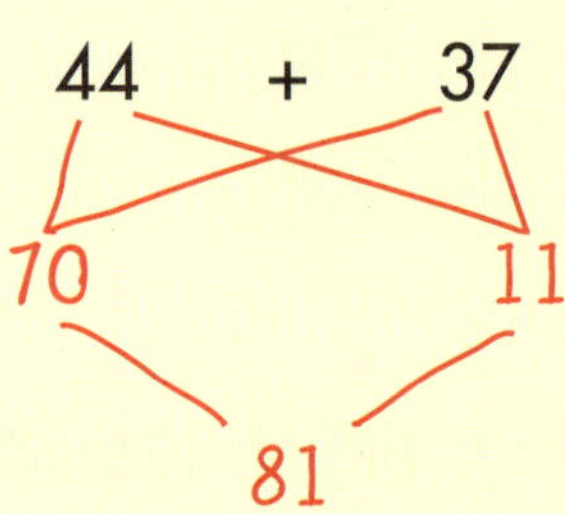

Show how to add 44 + 37 using an empty number line.

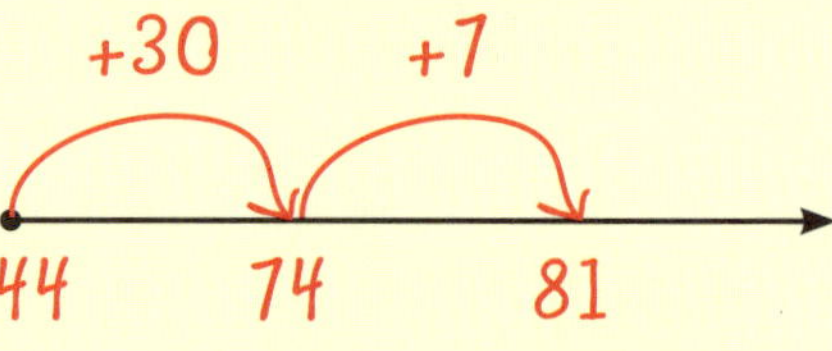

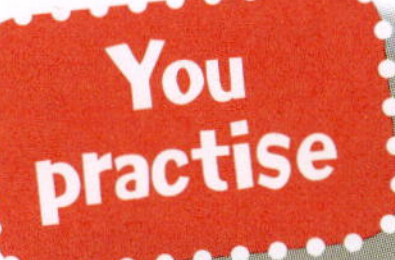

Show how to work out each addition using chunking.

27 + 34

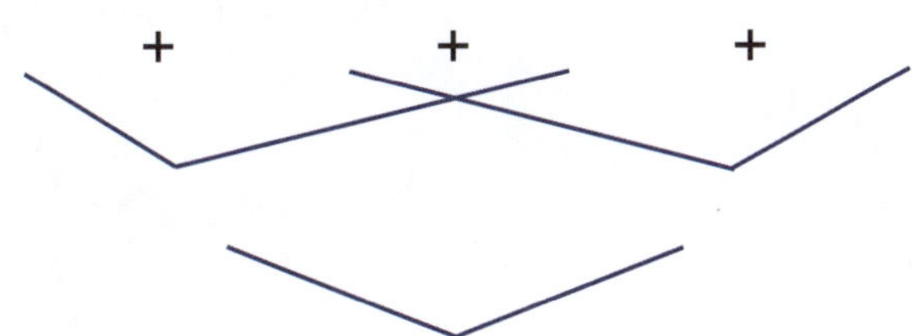

38 + 25

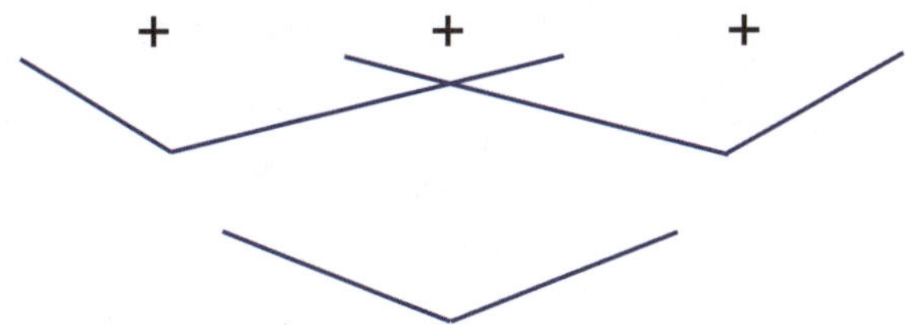

79 + 88

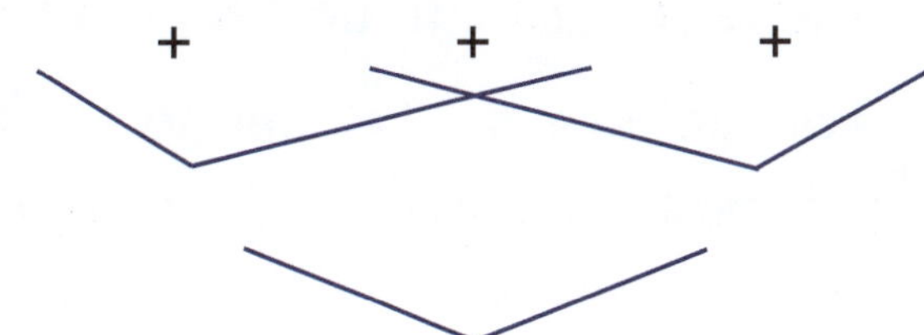

53 + 28

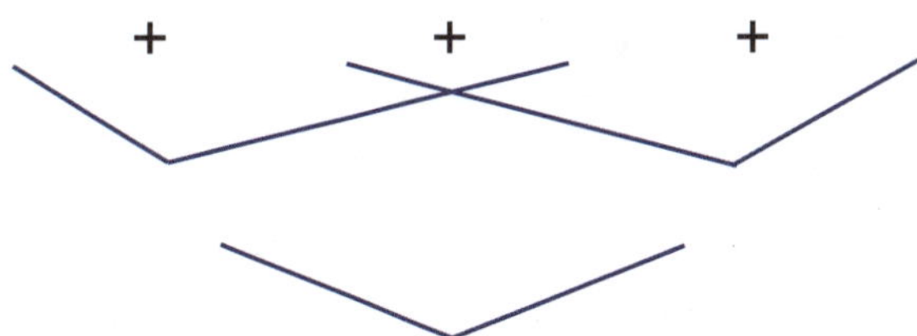

You practise

Show how to work out each addition using an empty number line.

18 + 36

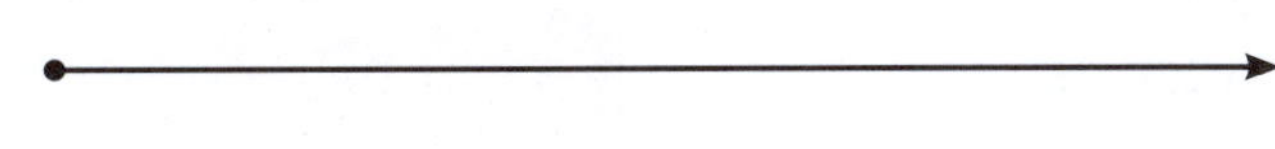

24 + 45

56 + 43

BOB time!

CHANGE THE ORDER

When you have to add more than two numbers, you can change the order of the numbers to make it easier to add them together.

For example, to work out **36 + 18 + 24**, you could just add these in this order or you could **reorder** the numbers so that pairs that add to 10 are together and use **chunking** to get the answer.

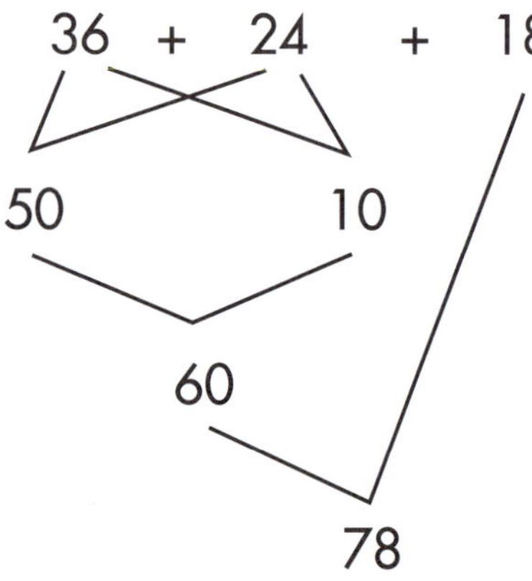

chunk 36 and 24 first

then add 18 onto the friendly number 60

It's fun to find smart ways to add.

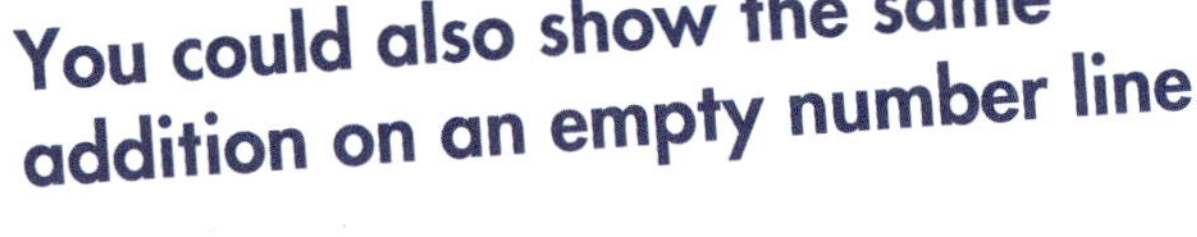

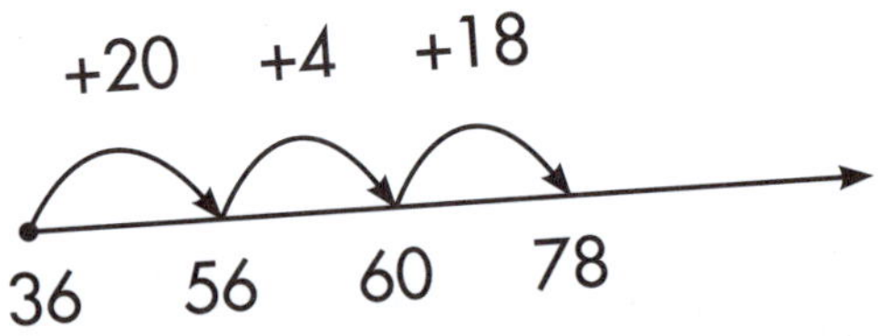

We practise

Reorder the numbers in 23 + 46 + 17 to make it easier to add them together. Show the addition as chunking.

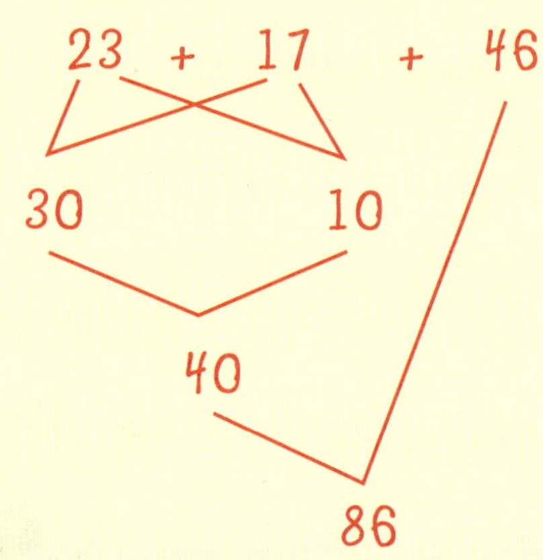

Reorder the numbers in 25 + 36 + 35 to make it easier to add them together. Show the addition on an empty number line.

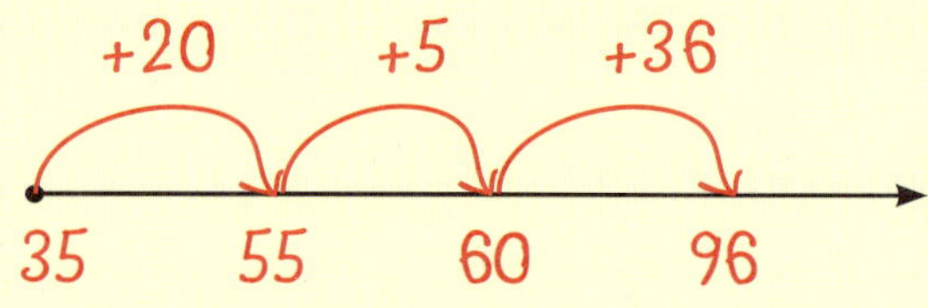

You practise

Reorder the numbers to make it easier to add them together. Show each addition as chunking.

27 + 36 + 14

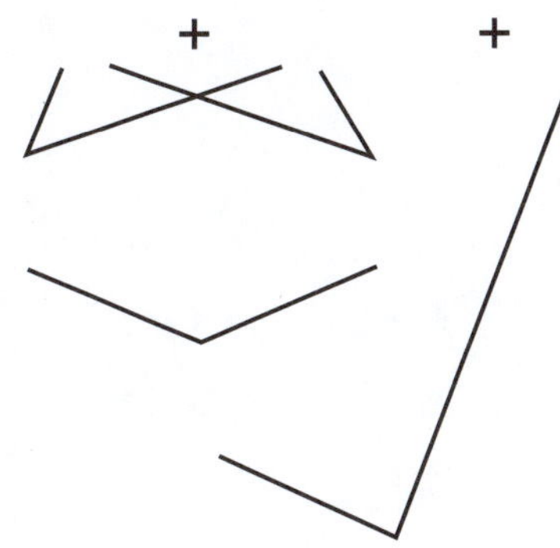

29 + 23 + 41

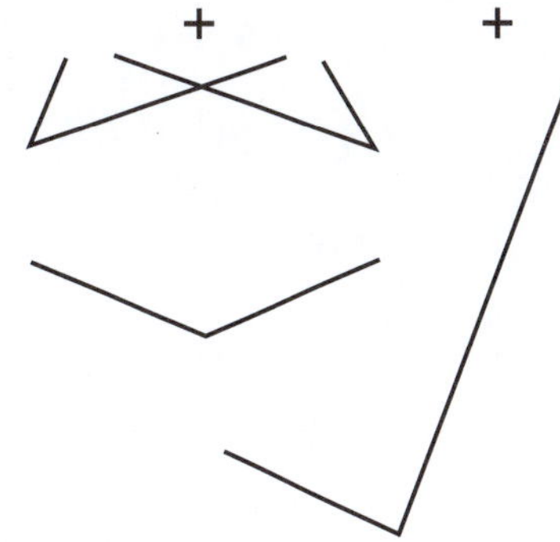

33 + 12 + 48

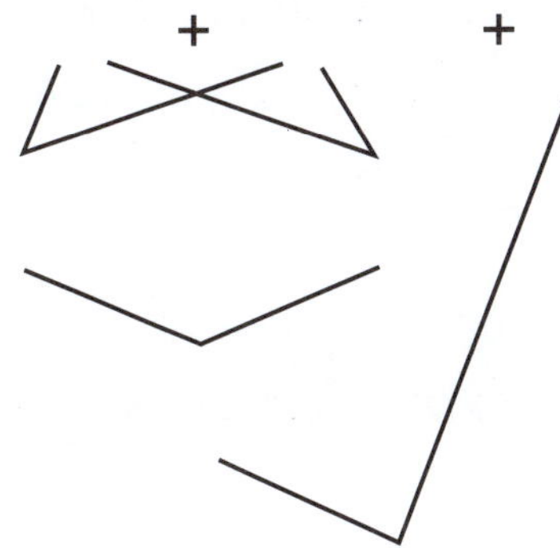

19 + 43 + 21

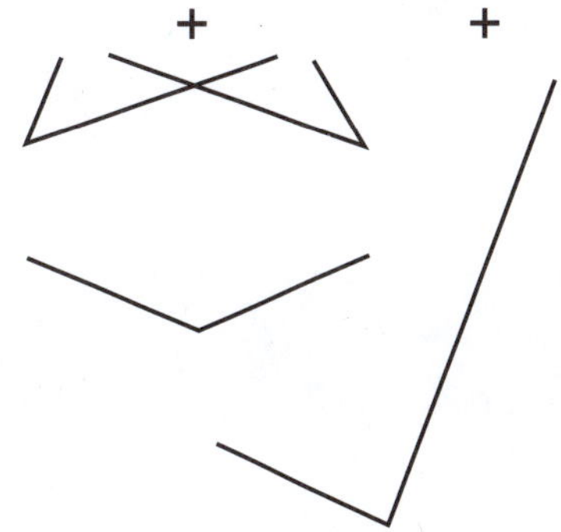

You practise

Reorder the numbers to make it easier to add them together. Show each addition on an empty number line.

28 + 16 + 32

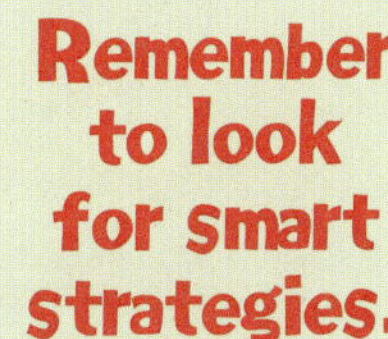

34 + 27 + 33

BOB time!

SUBTRACTING 10s

Subtracting numbers that end in a zero is easy. For example, if you don't instantly know the answer to 80 – 30, it can be solved by **counting back** in 10s.

80 70 60 50

80 – 30 = 50

It is easy to see the three jumps backwards when you show it on an empty number line.

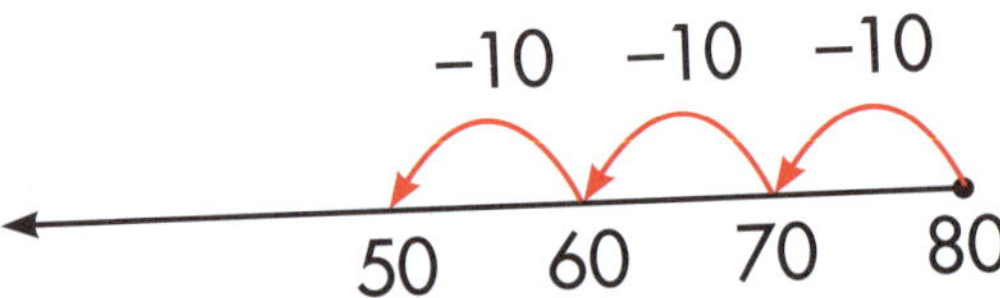

Sometimes you can use a smart strategy for subtracting. For example, to find **60 – 30** use **doubles**.

Double 30 is 60 (30 + 30 = 60)

60 – 30 = 30

You can also do this by counting back on an empty number line.

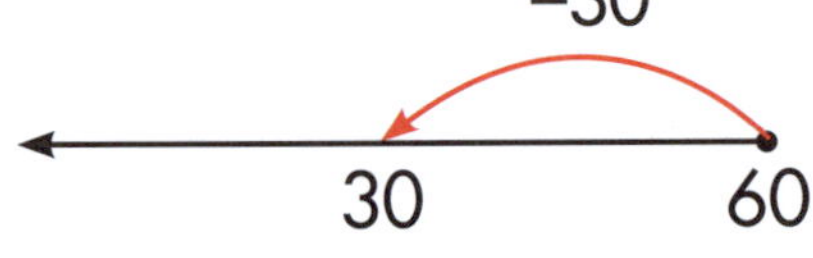

You could also use **near doubles**. For example, to find **75 – 30** you know the near double 30 + 40 = 70 and then 30 + 45 = 75, so 75 – 30 = 45.

We practise

Work out 70 – 20 by counting back on an empty number line.

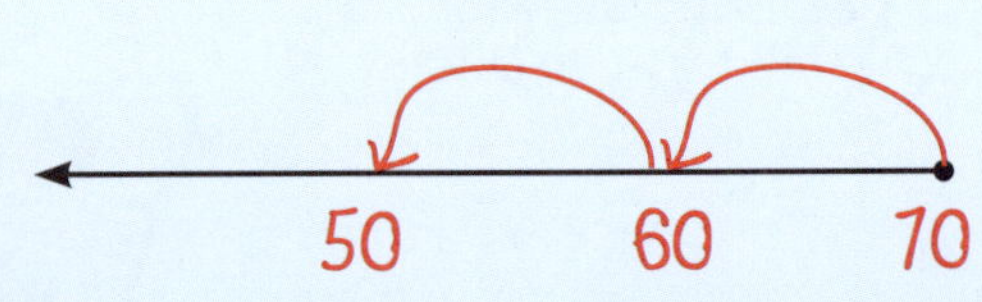

Which strategy would you use for 60 – 30?

Doubles

Do this subtraction on an empty number line.

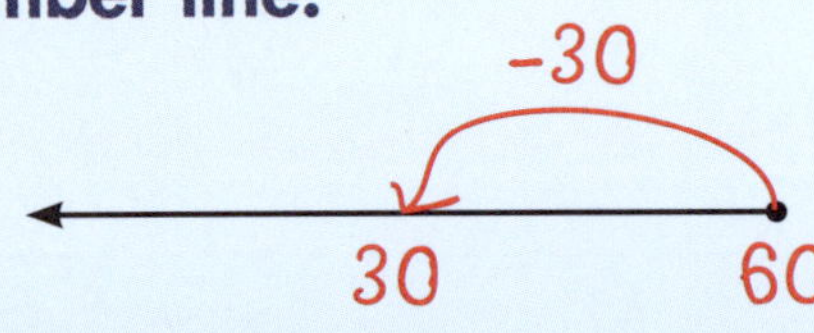

You practise

Do each subtraction by counting back on an empty number line.

1 70 – 20

2 80 – 30

3 95 – 30

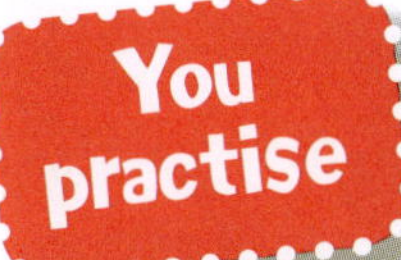

Which strategy would you use for each subtraction? Do each one on an empty number line.

4 40 – 20 ________________ strategy

Look out for doubles and near doubles.

5 55 – 20 ________________ strategy

6 96 – 50 ________________ strategy

UNIT 15

SUBTRACTING 10s and 1s

You know how to subtract 1s and you know how to subtract 10s, so now it is time to put them both together.

For example, you can work out **45 – 21** in your head by **number splitting**.

First **split** 21 into 20 and 1, then subtract 20 and then subtract 1 more.

45 – 20 = 25

25 – 1 = 24 so

45 – 21 = 24

This is how it looks on an empty number line.

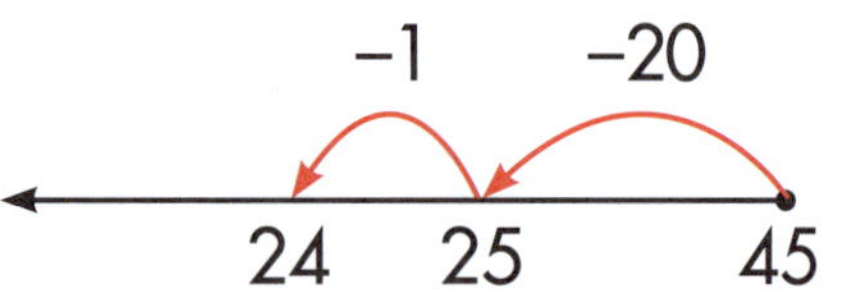

Some subtractions are not so easy, but they can still be done in your head.

For example, to work out **45 – 26** first **split** 26 into 20 and 6 and then subtract 20 to get 25.

Then to work out 25 – 6 you can use the **bridge** (except that this time you are bridging **back** through 20). It looks like this on an empty number line.

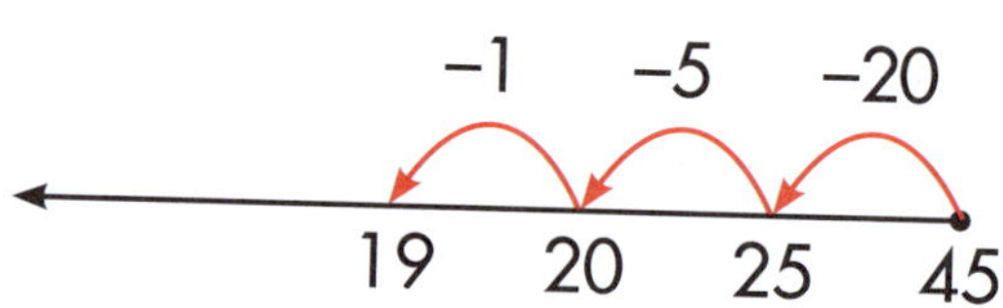

That's easy – I can do that in my head!

We practise

Use number splitting to work out these subtractions and then complete the empty number lines.

58 – 34

58 – 30 – 4 = 24

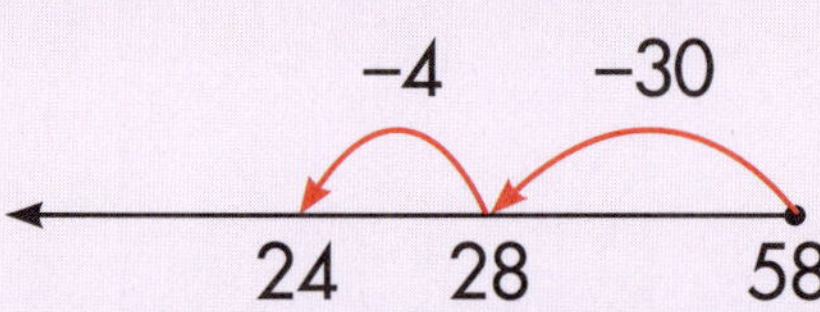

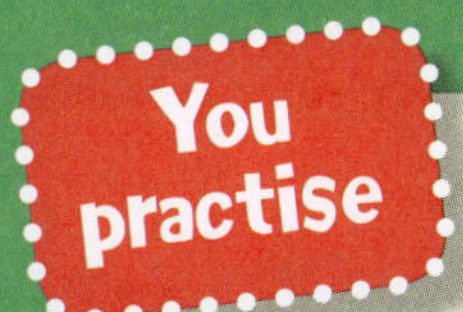

Use number splitting to work out each subtraction and then complete the empty number line.

65 – 43 ____ – ____ – ____ = ____

48 – 22 ____ – ____ – ____ = ____

67 – 35 ____ – ____ – ____ = ____

Look back through the book to find a strategy that will help with subtractions like these.

105 – 24 ____ – ____ – ____ = ____

34 – 15 ____ – ____ – ____ = ____

73 – 15 ____ – ____ – ____ = ____

UNIT 16

THE EQUALS SIGN

Many people think that the equals sign means makes altogether.

For example, they see the number sentence **3 + 4 =** and only think of the answer 7.

In fact, **3 + 4** can also be equal to **2 + 5**, or **1 + 6** or **10 – 3**. The equals sign actually means **is the same as** or **balances**.

If you put 10 on one side of the balance and 4 + 5 on the other side, it would not balance. You have to take 1 away from the 10 for it to balance.

The easiest way to think of this is to think of a **pan balance**. The numbers on the left side of the pan balance add to the same total as the numbers on the right side.

3 + 6 = 4 + 5

We practise

Complete these number sentences to make them balance.

2 + 4 = 1 + 5

5 + 2 = 8 – 1

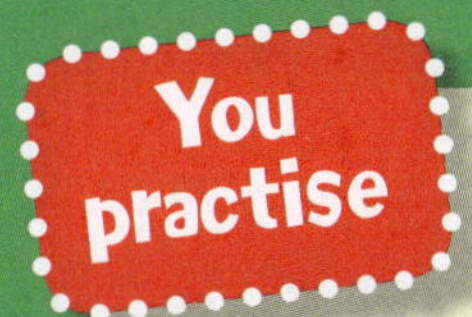

Complete each number sentence to make it balance.

3 + 3 = 2 + ____

2 + ____ = 3 + 5

9 + 4 = ____ + 10

____ + 3 = 10 − 3

10 + 4 = ____ − 6

6 + 3 = 11 − ____

____ − 5 = 13 − 4

8 + 6 = 20 − ____

9. 17 + 5 = ____ − 6

3 + ____ = 14 − 6

BOB time!

ADDITION and SUBTRACTION PATTERNS

Can you spot a pattern in this number sequence?

2 4 6 8 10 12 ...

It is easy to spot the pattern because there are only even numbers with 2 added each time. What about this one?

1 3 5 7 9 11 ...

It is another counting-in-2s sequence, but this time it starts on 1 and only has odd numbers.

You can do count-back patterns too.

Not all patterns are that easy to spot. Look at this one.

2 3 5 8 12 17 ...

There is a strategy to help with this one, as you can see below.

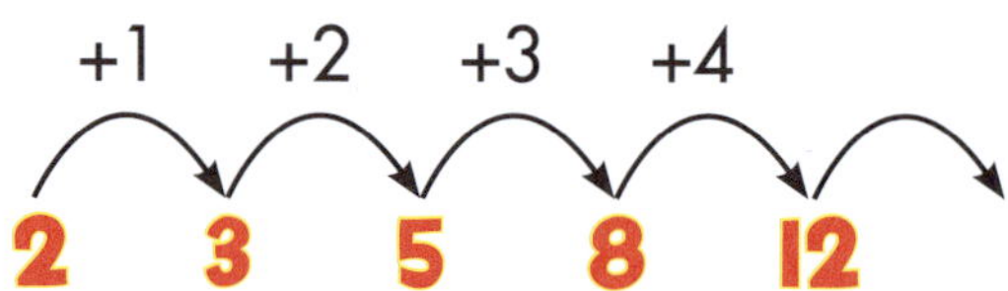

The next jump in the pattern is +5, so the next number is 17.

We practise

Continue this count-on sequence. Label the jumps to show the pattern.

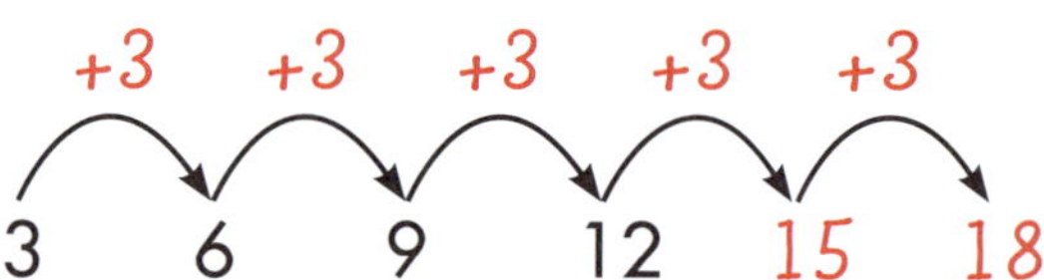

Continue this count-back sequence. Label the jumps to show the pattern.

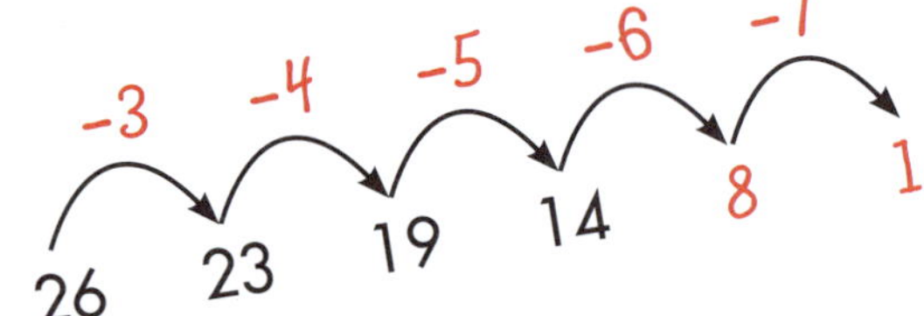

You practise

Continue each count-on sequence and label the jumps to show the pattern.

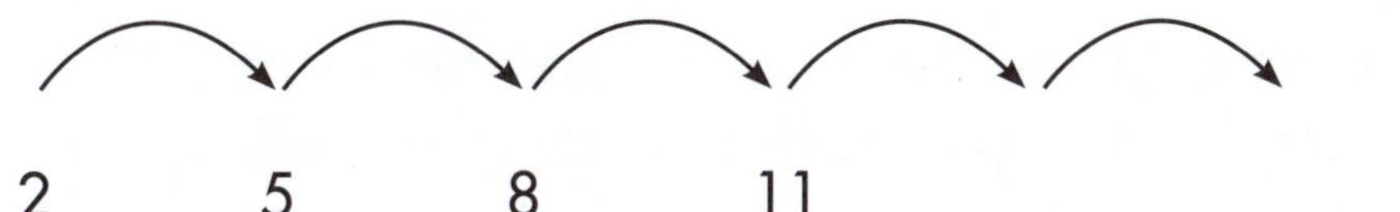

2 5 8 11 ____ ____

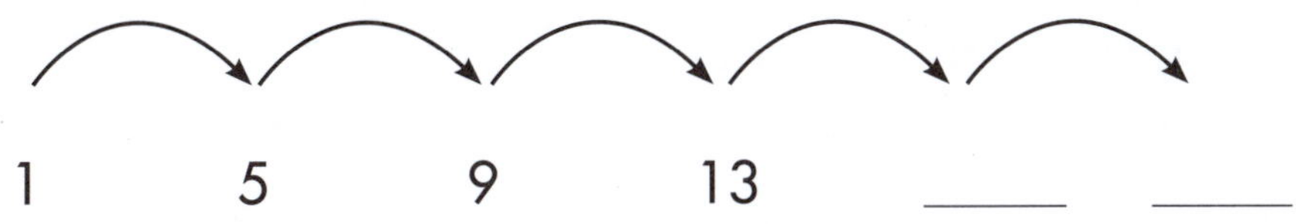

1 5 9 13 ____ ____

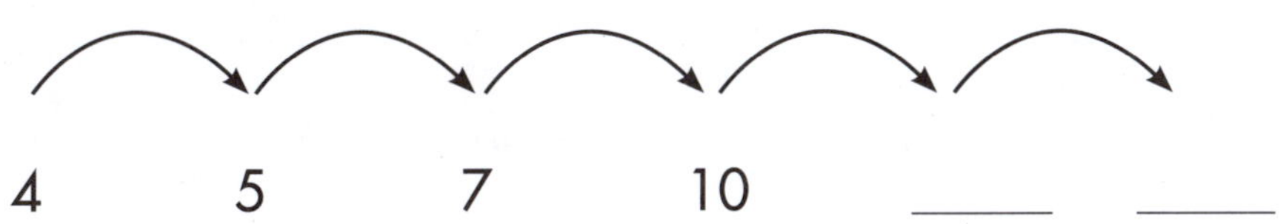

4 5 7 10 ____ ____

Continue each count-back sequence and label the jumps to show the pattern.

31 29 27 25 ____ ____

5. 43 39 35 31 ____ ____

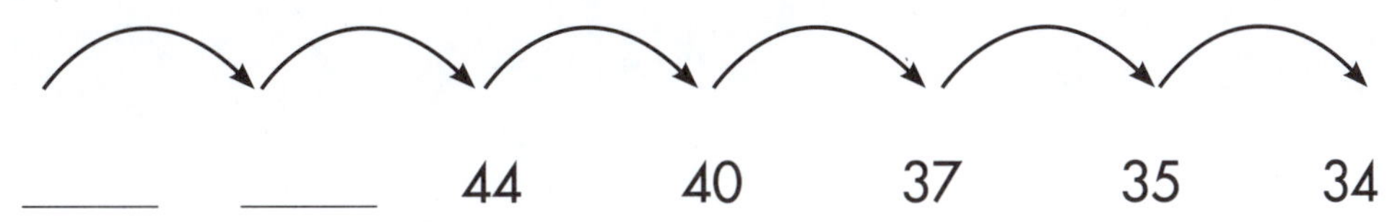

____ ____ 44 40 37 35 34

BOB time!

STRATEGIES for LARGER NUMBERS

In the additions below the numbers are larger than 10, but the strategies that you have already learnt still apply.

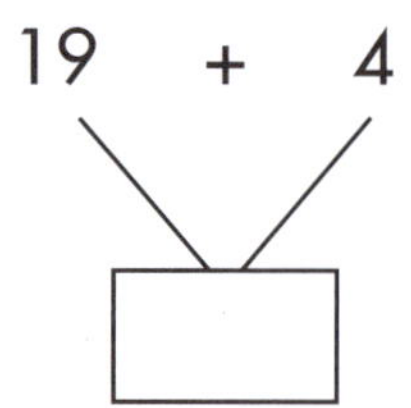

To find the value of the unknown **result**, you could use the **bridge strategy**, but this time bridge through 20 to find the answer 23.

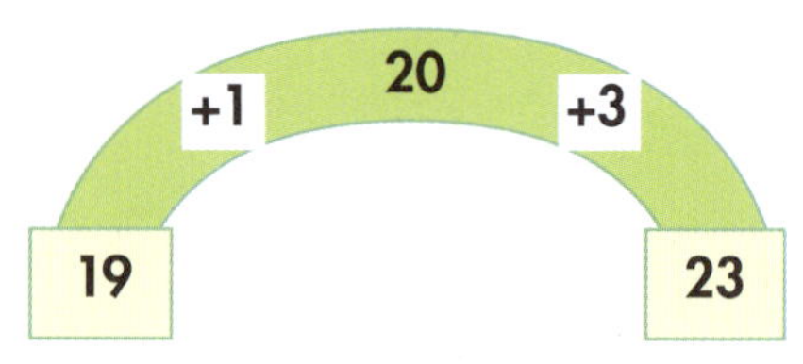

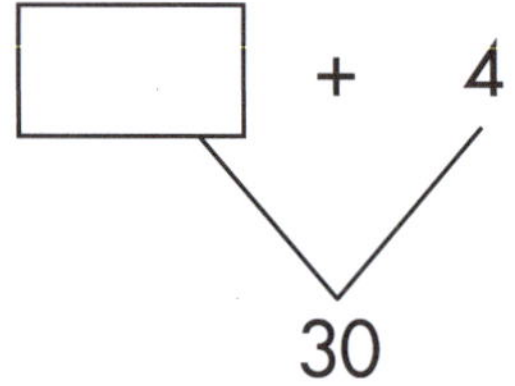

To find the value of the unknown **start**, you could use the **rainbow facts** because 6 + 4 = 10 and so 26 + 4 = 30.

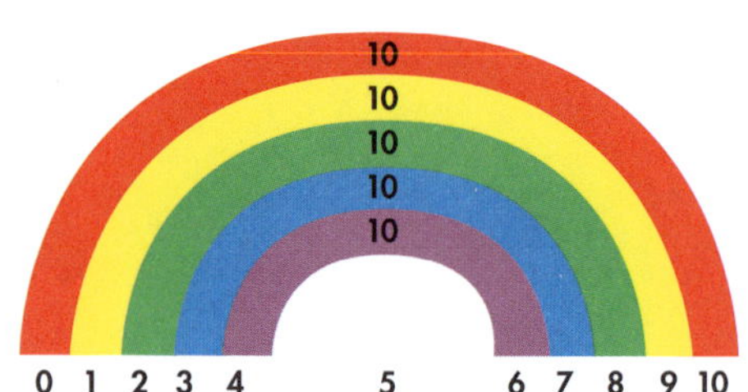

There is also a strategy to help you with subtraction with numbers larger than 10.

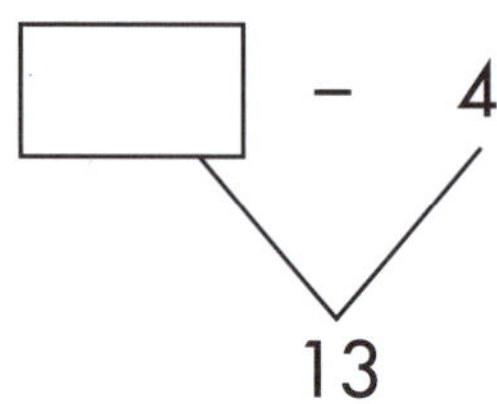

To find the value of the unknown start, you could count on 4 from 13 on a number line.

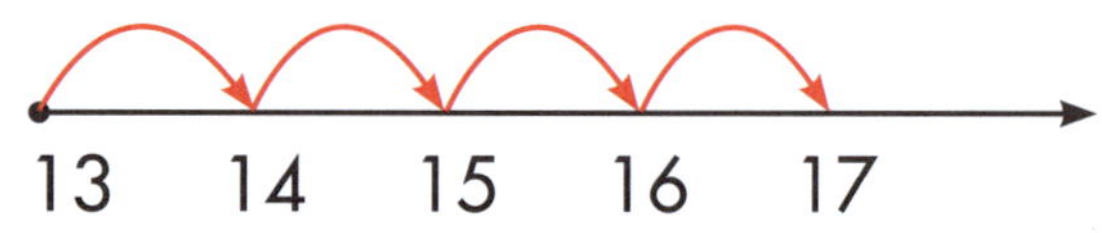

The subtraction is 17 – 4 = 13

Find the unknown in these examples.

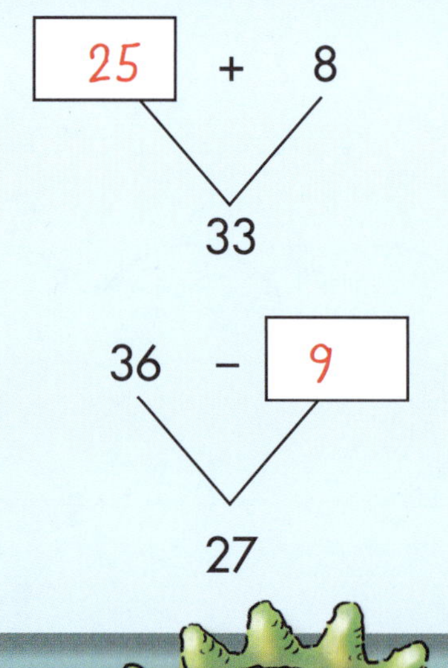

You practise

Find the unknown in each example.

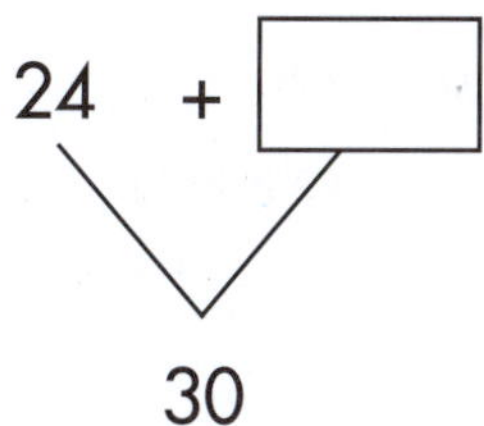

Don't get caught out! Check to see if it is an addition or a subtraction.

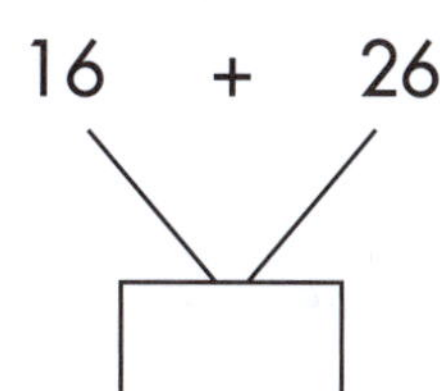

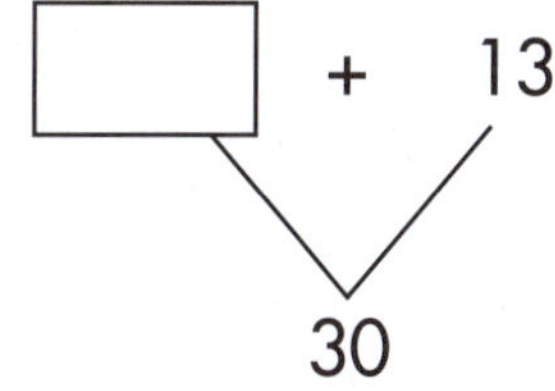

☐ + 18

36

48 − ☐

23

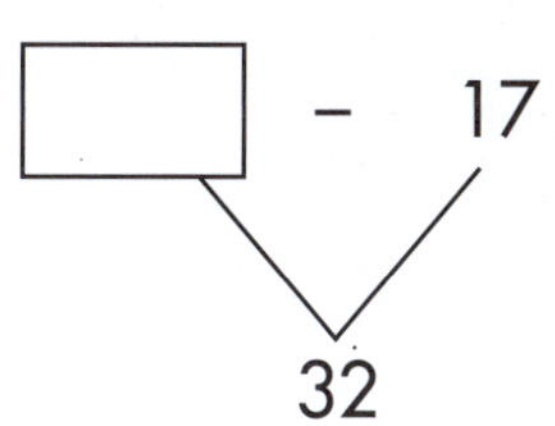

BOB time!

ROUND AND ADJUST

Now that you know about friendly numbers and can bridge through 10, you are ready to round and adjust.

But first you need to know how to **round** a number to its **nearest 10**.

The rule is that numbers that end in 1, 2, 3 and 4 **round down** to the 10 below, while numbers that end in 5, 6, 7, 8 and 9 **round up** to the 10 above.

0 1 2 3 4 5 6 7 8 9 10

Here are some examples:

19 rounds up to 20
39 rounds up 40
45 rounds up to 50
13 rounds down to 10
34 rounds down to 30
41 rounds down to 40

For **19 + 46** you could round 19 up to 20, which is a friendly number, and then add 46 to get 66.

But wait a minute! You added 1 to 19 to make 20 so you need to subtract 1 from 66 to get the correct answer, which is 65.

19 + 46

19 + 1 = 20 **round** 19 **up** to 20

20 + 46 = 66

66 – 1 = 65 **adjust** by subtracting 1

Round these numbers (up or down) to the nearest 10.

18 rounds up to 20

24 rounds down to 20

35 rounds up to 40

Show how to round and adjust to work out 28 + 15.

28 + 15

28 + 2 = 30

Round 30 + 15 = 45

Adjust 45 – 2 = 43

You practise Round each number (up or down) to the nearest 10.

1. 48 rounds __________ to ______

2. 72 rounds __________ to ______

3. 45 rounds __________ to ______

Rounding changes a number into a friendly number and friendly numbers are easy to add.

You practise Show how to round and adjust to work out each addition.

4. **29 + 17**

29 + _____ = _____

Round _____ + _____ = _____

Adjust _____ − _____ = _____

5. **38 + 26**

38 + _____ = _____

Round _____ + _____ = _____

Adjust _____ − _____ = _____

6. **42 + 79**

42 − _____ = _____

Round _____ + _____ = _____

Adjust _____ + _____ = _____

MORE PROBLEM SOLVING

Race Back from 100 is a game that Clare and Jake like to play.

On their turn they take two playing cards from the top of a pile and use them to make a 2-digit number score, which they subtract from their total. The first person to get back to zero or the last person to bust wins.

Clare has already scored 23 and 37. Jake has scored 18 and 41.

After subtracting their scores from 100, what numbers are Clare and Jake each on?

Notice that the important information is highlighted in blue and what has to be found out is highlighted in pink.

One way to work out the answer is to count back on a number line.

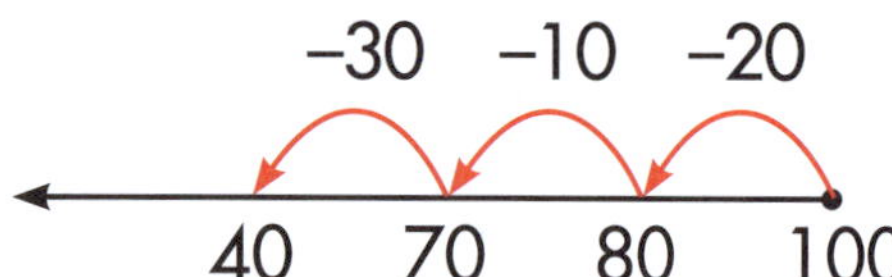

Clare added the second digit in each number, 3 and 7, to make 10 and then counted back in 10s.

−9 −40 −10

41 50 90 100

Jake added the second digit in each number, 8 and 1, to make 9 and then subtracted the 10 and 40 before subtracting the 9.

Answer: Clare is on 40 and Jake is on 41.

We practise

Highlight the important information and what you have to find out in this problem and then work out the answer.

Jake scored 54 after his first turn in Race Back from 100. What number is he on now?

Show your solution on an empty number line.

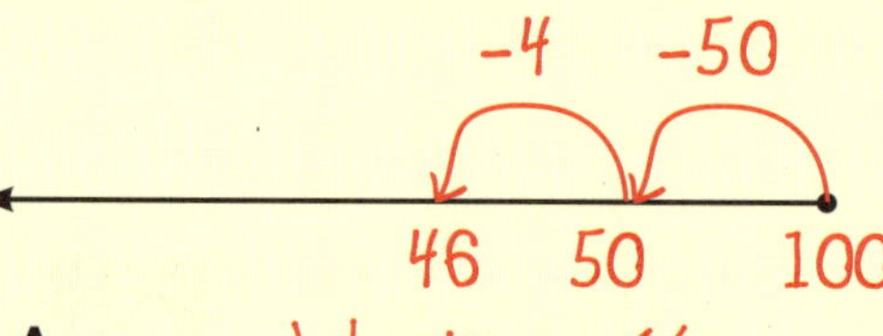

Answer: Jake is on 46

Remember to write the answer as a sentence.

You practise

Highlight the important information and solve the problems using chunking or an empty number line.

1. Clare and Matty are playing a card game called Largest Total Wins. Clare drew 4, 7 and 6, Matty drew 5, 3 and 9. Who has the larger total?

____

2. Clare's first two cards were a 3 and 6. After taking the third card, her total score was 17. What was her third card? _______________

3. Jake scored 24 with three cards and won the game. Matty had 3, 6 and 7. How much did Jake win by? _______________

4. The baker made a tray of 48 buns. He put 12 into a box for the coffee shop and 18 in the display case. How many buns does he have left?

____

5. Jake had $64 for shopping. He spent $20 and then $15. How much money does he have left? _______________

6. Clare spent $45 and $16. How much money does she have left from the $100 that she started with? _______________

7. Matty was playing darts. He threw double 6, 25 and 13 with his three darts. What is his score? _______________

8. Matty is playing darts and needs 53 points to win. He throws double 12, 10 and 15. How many more points does Matty need? _______________

9. Clare, Jake and Matty are collecting fallen apples. Clare has 24, Jake has 10 more than Clare and Matty has 29. How many apples do they have altogether?

____

10. Clare's class did a survey about pets. They found that the class has 18 dogs, 9 cats, 3 horses, 55 rabbits and 49 fish between them. How many pets does the class have altogether? _______________

BOB time!

TEST 1

1. There are 8 apples in a bowl and then 3 are eaten. How many are left?

____

2. Which doubles fact would help you find the answer to 4 + 5?

____

3. What is the number in the rainbow pair that goes with 3 to make 10?

____

4. What is 20 + 4?

____

5. What strategy could you use to work out 10 – 6? What is the answer?

____

____

6. What near-double fact could help you to work out 7 – 4? What is the answer?

7. Complete the bridge to show how to work out 8 + 6.

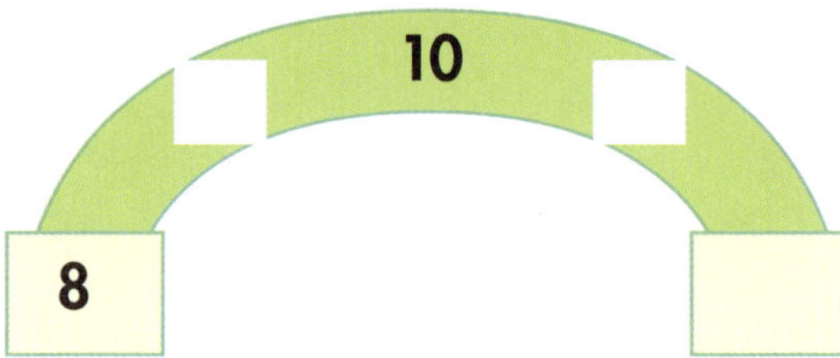

8. Rearrange the number string 3 + 5 + 4 + 7 and use chunking to find the total.

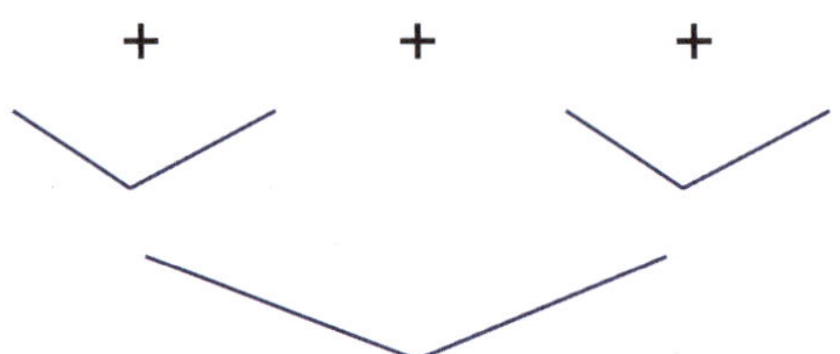

9. Complete this addition and write what is unknown.

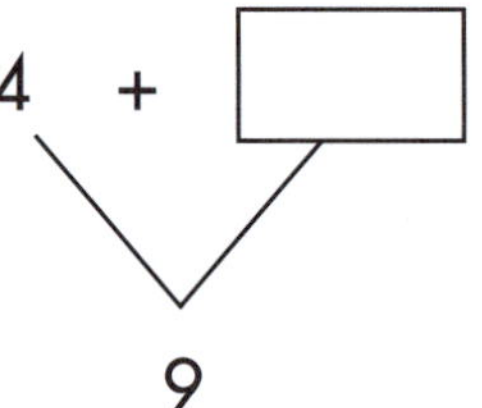

The ______________ is unknown

10. Matt ate 7 cherries and had 5 cherries left. How many cherries did he start with? Complete the diagram to solve the problem.

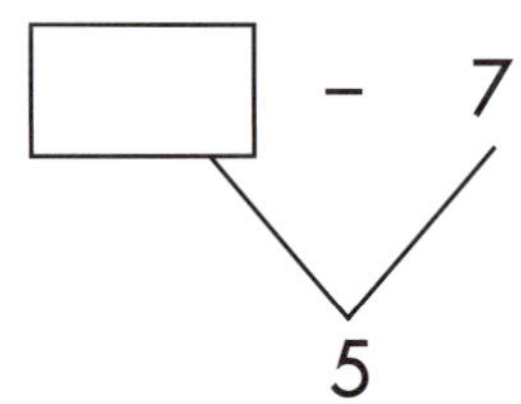

____

TEST 2

What is 30 + 18?

____

Show how to add 35 + 28 using chunking.

35 + 28

___ ___

___

Reorder 35 + 18 + 25 to make them easy to add.

___ + ___ + ___

___ ___

___

Work out 38 + 26 using an empty number line.

Work out 73 – 30 by counting back on an empty number line.

Use number splitting to work out 45 – 26 and then complete the empty number line.

____

Make this number sentence balance.

4 + 5 = 3 + ___

Continue this counting sequence and label the jumps.

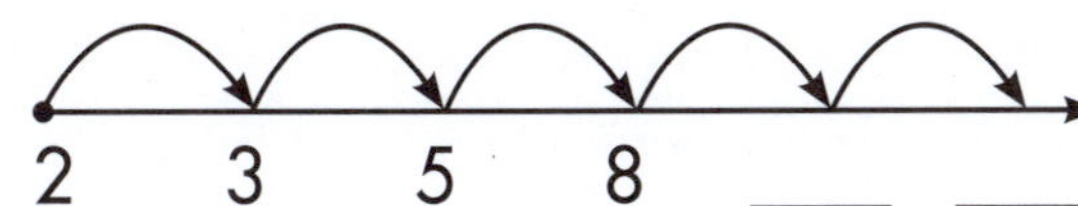

2 3 5 8 ___ ___

Find the unknown in this subtraction.

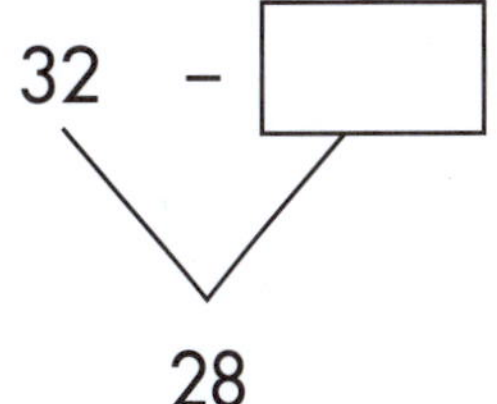

32 – [ ]

28

10. Clare is saving for a \$50 phone card. She saved \$12 in the first week and \$22 in the second week. How much more does she need to save? Show the answer on an empty number line.

____

ANSWERS

Unit 1

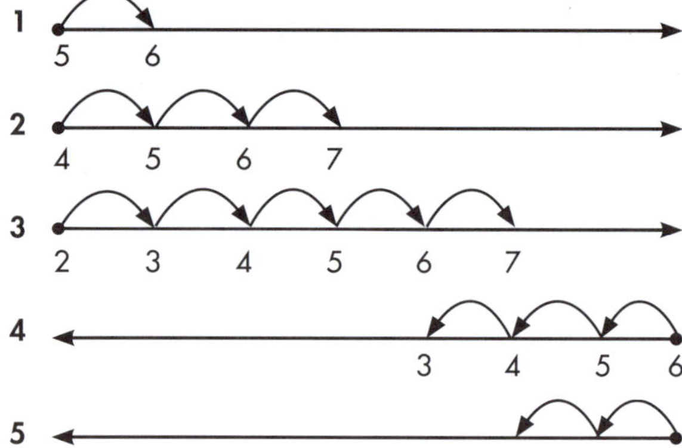

Unit 2

1 5 + 5 = 10
2 4 + 4 = 8
3 6 + 6 = 12
4 2 + 2 = 4
5 3 + 3 = 6
6 7 + 7 = 14
7 4 + 4 + 1 = 9
5 + 5 − 1 = 9
8 3 + 3 + 1 = 7
4 + 4 − 1 = 7
9 5 + 5 + 1 = 11
6 + 6 − 1 = 11
10 6 + 6 + 1 = 13
7 + 7 − 1 = 13

Unit 3

1	3 + 7 = 10	
2	1 + 9 = 10	
3	4 + 6 = 10	
4	2 + 8 = 10	
5	3 + 7 = 10	
6	0 + 10 = 10	10 + 0 = 10
7	3 + 7 = 10	7 + 3 = 10
8	2 + 8 = 10	8 + 2 = 10
9	4 + 6 = 10	6 + 4 = 10
10	1 + 9 = 10	9 + 1 = 10

Unit 4

1 5 + 0 = 5
2 8 + 0 = 8
3 3 + 0 = 3
4 0 + 4 = 4
5 0 + 6 = 6
6 10 + 6 = 16
7 10 + 9 = 19
8 8 + 20 = 28
9 4 + 30 = 34
10 50 + 3 = 53

Unit 5

1	10 − 3 = 7	
2	10 − 4 = 6	
3	10 − 1 = 9	
4	10 − 2 = 8	
5	20 − 4 = 16	
6	10 − 8 = 2	2 + 8 = 10
7	20 − 3 = 17	7 + 3 = 10
8	30 − 6 = 24	4 + 6 = 10
9	40 − 9 = 31	1 + 9 = 10
10	50 − 7 = 43	3 + 7 = 10

Unit 6

1	10 − 5 = 5	5 + 5 = 10
2	6 − 3 = 3	3 + 3 = 6
3	12 − 6 = 6	6 + 6 = 12
4	14 − 7 = 7	7 + 7 = 14
5	20 − 10 = 10	10 + 10 = 20
6	5 − 2 = 3	2 + 3 = 5
7	9 − 4 = 5	4 + 5 = 9
8	11 − 6 = 5	5 + 6 = 11
9	19 − 9 = 10	9 + 10 = 19
10	21 − 10 = 11	10 + 11 = 21

Unit 7

1

2
+3 10 +2
7 12

3

4

5

6

Unit 8

1 2 + 8 + 7 + 1
10 8
18

2
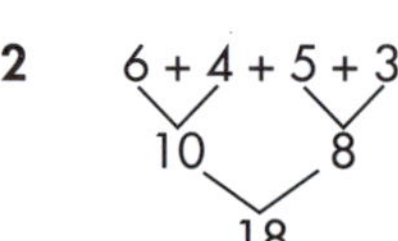

ANSWERS

3 9 + 1 + 7 + 2
10 9
19

4 7 + 3 + 6 + 1
10 7
17

5 3 + 4 + 8 + 5
7 13
20

6 3 + 4 + 5 + 2
7 7
14

7 7 + 2 + 4 + 5
9 9
18

8 3 + 6 + 9 + 5
9
18
23

Unit 9

1 3
2 3
3 11
4 8 the change is unknown
5 28 the result is unknown
6 8 the start is unknown

Unit 10

1 There are 22 pencils altogether.
2 Matty has 6 marbles left.
3 The chickens laid 20 eggs altogether.
4 Clare's mum has 4 apples left.
5 There are 7 apples in the other bowl.
6 Clare has 6 marbles left.
7 The baker needs 8 more eggs.
8 Matty won the game with 21.
9 Clare won by 2.
10 Clare spent $16.

Unit 11

1 60 Count on
2 100 Rainbow fact
3 80 Double
4 90 Near double
5 40 Near double
6 36
7 77
8 15
9 6
10 50

Unit 12

1 50 + 11 = 61
2 50 + 13 = 63
3 150 + 17 = 167

4
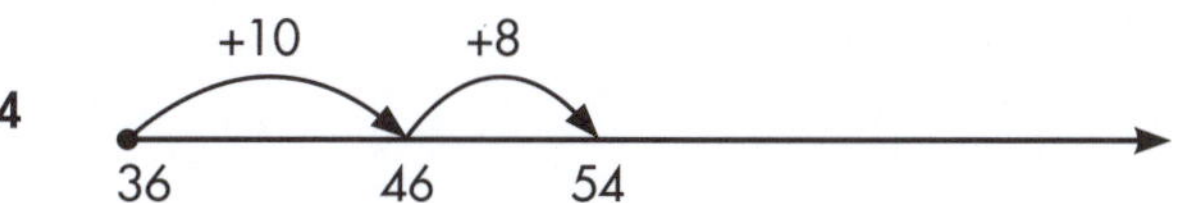

5
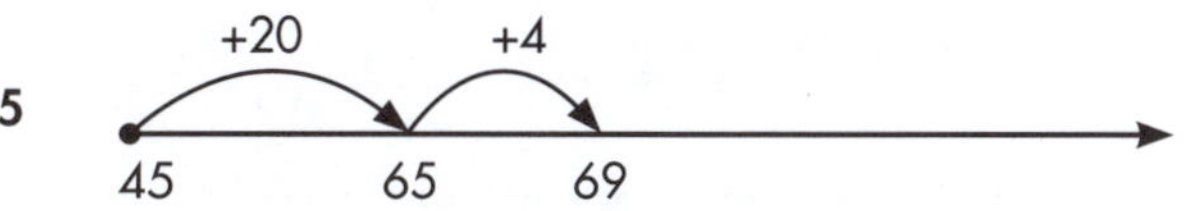

6
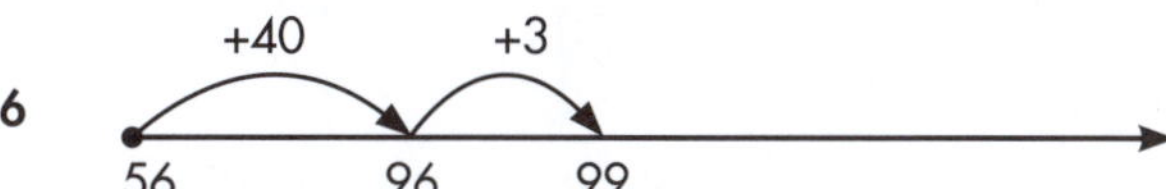

Unit 13

1 36 + 14 + 27
40 10
50
77

2 29 + 41 + 23
60 10
70
93

3 12 + 48 + 33
50 10
60
93

4
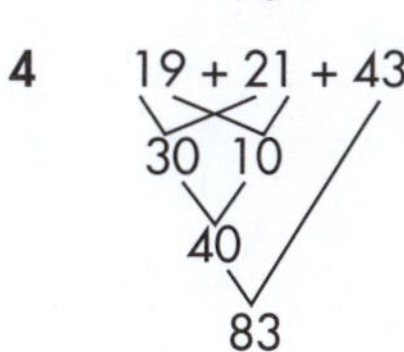

ANSWERS

5

+8 +20 +16

32 40 60 76

6

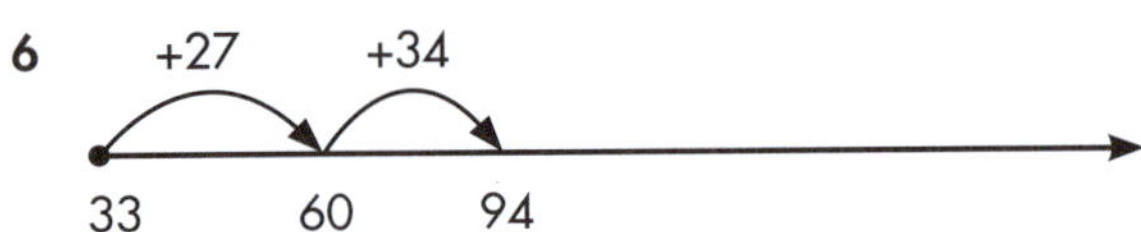

Unit 14

1, 2, 3

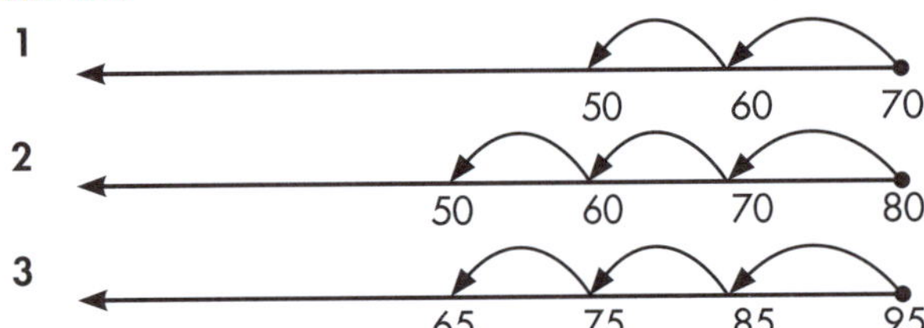

4 doubles strategy

5 counting back strategy

6 near doubles strategy

Unit 15

1 65 – 40 – 3 = 22

2 48 – 20 – 2 = 26

3 67 – 30 – 5 = 32

4 105 – 20 – 4 = 81

5 34 – 10 – 5 = 19

6 73 – 10 – 5 = 58

Unit 16

1 3 + 3 = 2 + 4
2 2 + 6 = 3 + 5
3 9 + 4 = 3 + 10
4 4 + 3 = 10 – 3
5 10 + 4 = 20 – 6
6 6 + 3 = 11 – 2
7 14 – 5 = 13 – 4
8 8 + 6 = 20 – 6
9 17 + 5 = 28 – 6
10 3 + 5 = 14 – 6

Unit 17

1

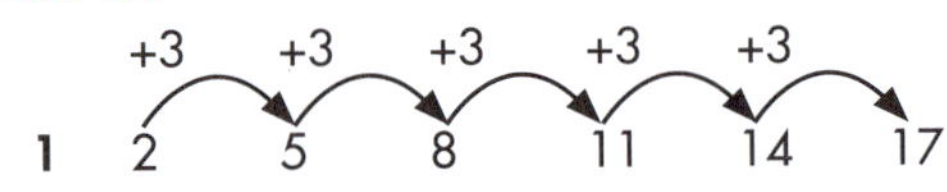

2

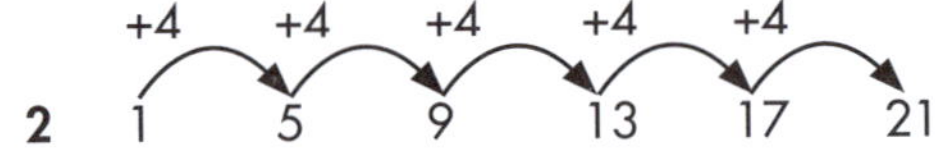

3

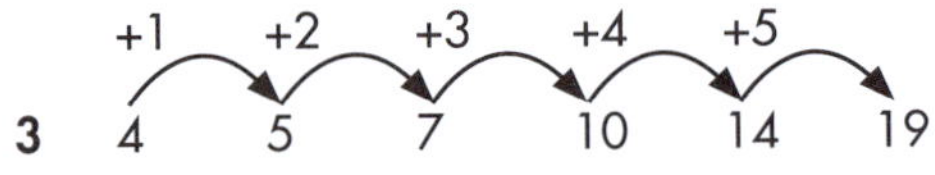

4

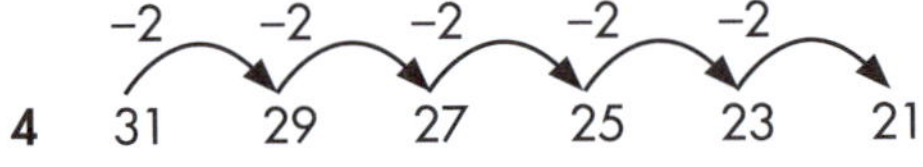

5

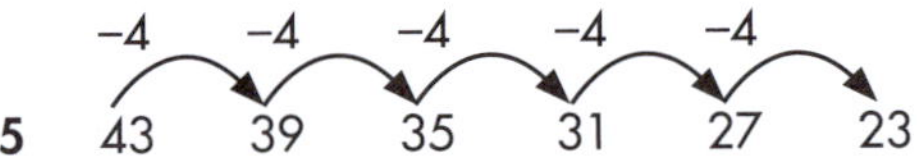

6

−6 −5 −4 −3 −2 −1

55 49 44 40 37 35 34

Unit 18

1

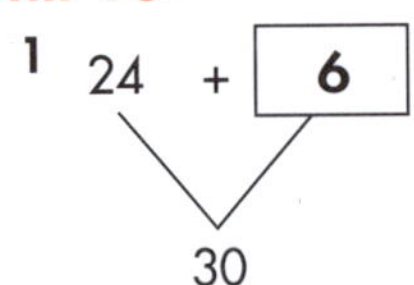

2

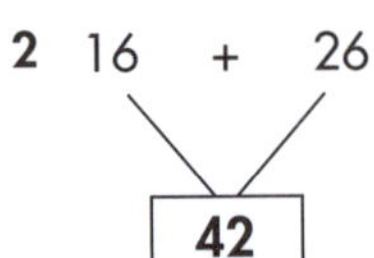

3

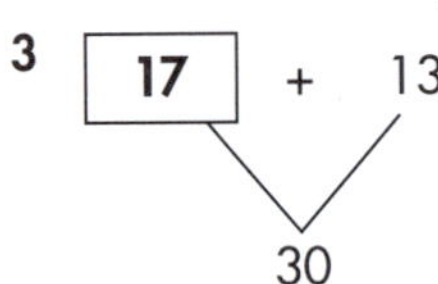

4

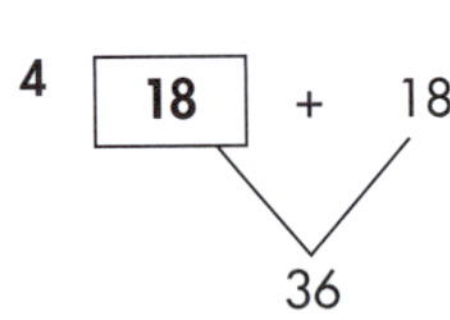

5
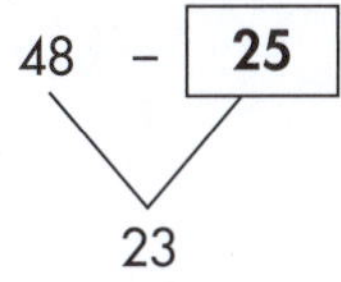

6
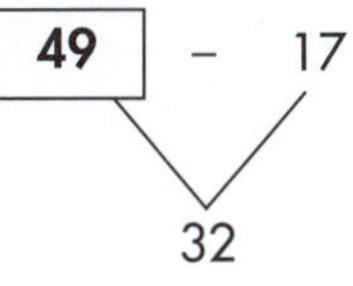

Unit 19

1 48 rounds up to 50
2 72 rounds down to 70
3 45 rounds up to 50
4 29 + 1 = 30
Round 30 + 17 = 47
Adjust 47 – 1 = 46
5 38 + 2 = 40
Round 40 + 26 = 66
Adjust 66 – 2 = 64
6 42 – 2 = 40
Round 40 + 79 = 119
Adjust 119 + 2 = 121

Unit 20

1 They both have a total of 17.
2 Her third card was 8.
3 Jake won by 8.
4 The baker has 18 buns left.
5 Jake has $29 left.
6 Clare has $39 left.
7 Matty's score is 50
8 Matty needed 4 points to win.
9 They have 87 apples altogether.
10 The class has 134 pets altogether.

Test 1

1 5
2 4 + 4
3 7
4 24
5 rainbow fact 4
6 3 + 4 3

7 14
+2 10 +4
8 14

8 7 + 3 + 5 + 4
10 9
19

9 4 + 5
9
The change is unknown.

10 12 – 7
5
There were 12 cherries to start with.

Test 2

1 48
2 50 + 13 = 63
3
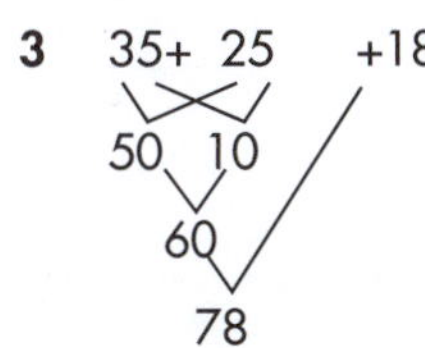

4
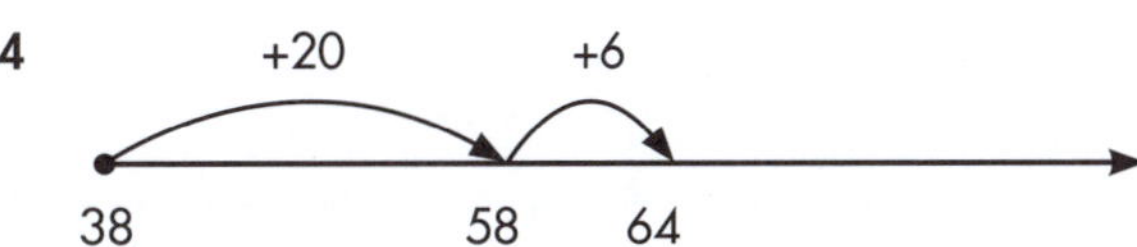

5
43 53 63 73

6 45 – 20 – 6 = 19
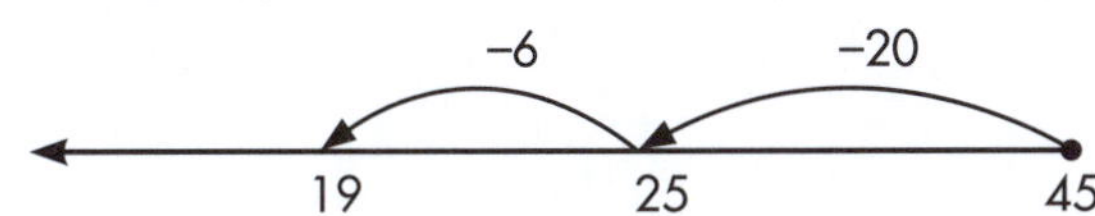

7 6

8
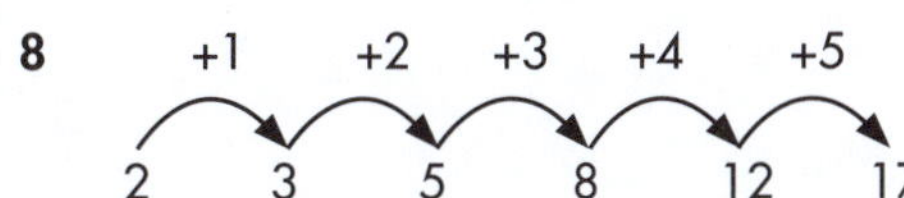

9 4

10
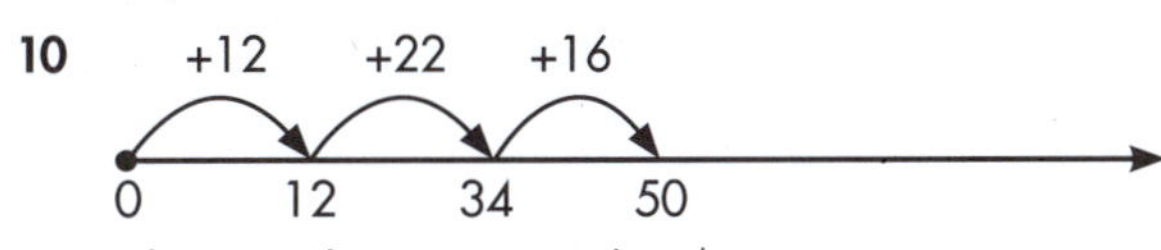

Clare needs to save another $16.

Back to Basics Addition and Subtraction Years 2–3

Reprinted 2015, 2018, 2024

ISBN: 978 1 74215 930 0

Published by Pascal Press
PO Box 250
Glebe NSW 2037
www.pascalpress.com.au
contact@pascalpress.com.au

Author: Ann Baker
Publisher: Lynn Dickinson
Editor: Eliza Hope
Proofreader: Tim Learner
Design and illustration: Janice Bowles
Cover design: Deb Snibson, MAPG
Printed by Wai Man Book Binding (China) Ltd.